Alice's Adventures

The Further Memoirs of a Cat

Alice's Adventures

The Further Memoirs of a Cat

Copyright © 1992 Alice

The right of Alice to be identified as author of this work has been asserted in accordance with the Copyright, Design and Patents Act 1988.

All rights reserved. No part of this publication may be reproduced, stored in a retrieval system, or transmitted in any form or by any means, electronic, mechanical, photocopying, recording or otherwise without prior permission of the publishers.

First published in 1992 by Chilton Designs, Publishing House, Trinity Place, Barnstaple, Devon, EX32 9HJ, England.

Reprinted 1999, 2002, 2008, 2009

This book is sold subject to the condition that it shall not be by way of trade or otherwise lent, re-sold, hired out or otherwise circulated without the publisher's prior consent in any form of binding or cover other than that in which it is published and without similar condition including this condition being imposed upon the subsequent purchaser

About the author

Alice is a 9 year old mixed tabby. She lives in Devon and shares her home with her half sister Thomasina and two Uprights. This is her second book. Her first book – "Alice's Diary" – has been hugely successful but Alice remains unchanged and her hobbies still include sleeping, eating and sitting in the sun.

Dedicated in sorrow to the memory of the thousands of cats and kittens who have died alone, in pain, in fear and without purpose in vivisection laboratories; in hope for the thousands more who wait, frightened and alone in cages; and in thanks to the many Uprights who are fighting to stop this cruel, pointless and inexcusably barbaric practice.

Alice

January 1st

Thomasina and I are convinced that something odd is going on.

It all began before dawn when I was woken by the alarm clock. I was, as usual, lying on the bottom of the Uprights' bed, and right from the moment the alarm started to ring I knew that it was going to be an unusual day.

Normally, the Uprights treat the alarm clock with undiluted disdain, but that didn't happen this morning. Instead of lying there and pretending to be asleep the Upright in Trousers leapt out of bed the moment the alarm started to ring.

Within minutes he and the Upright who wears a Skirt were washed and dressed and all four of us were downstairs eating our breakfasts. Normally, I like to approach breakfast in a leisurely fashion, having a stalk in the garden before I settle down to any serious eating, but the sense of urgency which had been steadily building since the alarm clock had rung was impossible to ignore and I knew instinctively that it was going to be a day I would want to forget as soon as possible.

As soon as the Uprights had finished their breakfast the Upright who wears a Skirt started washing up, and the moment Thomasina and I stopped eating our dish was picked up and taken over to the sink. Silently and anxiously Thomasina and I sat and watched the Uprights hurrying about.

While the Upright who wears a Skirt dried our dish the Upright in Trousers went outside and came back moments later clutching a huge pile of empty cardboard boxes. Without pausing he and the Upright who wears a Skirt immediately started to take things out of the kitchen cupboards and to put them into the boxes. Pots and pans were merely stacked one on top of the other, but anything that looked potentially breakable was wrapped in sheets of newspaper first.

"I disappeared upstairs and watched through the rails on the upstairs landing."

Neither Thomasina nor I had any idea what was going on but our sense of alarm was heightened an hour or so later by a loud banging on the back door. Thomasina darted out into the hall and I disappeared upstairs and watched through the rails on the landing.

There were three of them and the odd thing was that although they were complete strangers our Uprights seemed to be pleased to see them.

The oldest of the three strangers, a small Upright who wore a green boiler suit, took charge. His first act was to take the kettle out of one of the boxes and to hand it to the Upright who wears a Skirt. While she held it under the tap to fill it with water the Upright in Trousers plucked three newspaper wrapped parcels out of another card-board box, unwrapped them and placed three mugs on the kitchen table.

To say that I was puzzled by all this would be an understatement of heroic proportions. Our Uprights do occasionally have groups of visitors in the house but it is usually at the end of the day not the beginning. Besides, these strangers were not laughing or telling one another stories in the way that Uprights normally do when they are visiting. Everything seemed very serious and business-like.

I was so puzzled by what was going on that I very nearly didn't notice the Upright in Trousers moving towards me. As it was, I was far too slow and seconds later I found myself being picked up, carried along the landing and shut in the bathroom. A few moments later the bathroom door was opened a few inches and Thomasina was thrust unceremoniously in through the gap. Five minutes after that the Upright in Trousers returned with a litter tray which he placed on the floor by the side of the bath.

Although we were no longer able to see what was happening we could hear a lot of banging and bumping and scraping going on downstairs, and both Thomasina and I became increasingly alarmed as the day went on.

For a while Thomasina tried scratching at the bathroom door to attract attention but I warned her that I didn't think it would do any good.

In order to try and find somewhere warm and cosy for us both to settle down to sleep I knocked the top off the laundry basket, expecting to find the usual soft pile of clothes inside it. To my astonishment, the laundry basket was quite empty. With nowhere else to go Thomasina and I settled down together in the corner of the bathroom furthest from the door, and although we both tried hard to relax we found sleep quite elusive. I was only grateful that I had Thomasina for company. Being held prisoner in the bathroom was bad enough. To have been held prisoner alone would have been even worse.

When the Upright in Trousers and the Upright who wears a Skirt entered the bathroom several hours later both Thomasina and I were emotionally exhausted.

The Uprights had brought with them a bowlful of food, but although we were hungry Thomasina and I were both far too anxious to find food attractive so we didn't even move when they put the bowl down. After failing to encourage us to eat the Uprights both bent down. The Upright in Trousers picked me up and the Upright who wears a Skirt picked Thomasina up.

They cuddled us and then they carried us out of the bathroom.

The three strangers had disappeared but so had virtually everything else in the house. All the furniture had gone and the floorboards were bare. As we passed the bedroom door on our way to the staircase I noticed that even the bed and the wardrobe had vanished.

The house was empty!

Before I knew what was happening the Upright in Trousers had put me into a wicker basket and closed the lid. There was a metal grille at one end of the basket and through it I could see that the Upright who wears a Skirt had put Thomasina into another, similar basket. Moments later our baskets were picked up, carried outside and put on top of a pile of boxes and suitcases in the back of the Uprights' motor car. I could hear Thomasina but I couldn't see her, and I felt as frightened as she sounded.

After a few minutes our Uprights climbed into the car and slammed the doors behind them. It was a small comfort to know that wherever we were going, they were going with us.

"To my astonishment the laundry basket was empty."

After we had been travelling for a while I began to feel sick. Outside it was going dark but the car showed no signs of stopping. I had never been so frightened in my life. I lay down in the basket and tried to sleep.

January 2

I have no idea what time I fell asleep yesterday, or how far we eventually travelled, but I woke up sometime during the night to find that my basket was being lifted out of the back of the car and was being carried into a house I knew I had never visited before.

The night air was cold but was filled with a hundred new and pungent smells and the house, which seemed to be somewhere in the country, was surrounded by fields and trees.

When my basket was eventually lowered to the ground and the metal grille lifted I peered out cautiously before leaving it. The first thing I saw was Thomasina gingerly stepping out of her basket and looking anxiously in my direction.

"Where are we?" asked Thomasina. "What's happening?"

I looked around. "I've no idea," I told her. We were in a large, well lit room that contained no furniture and had no carpets on the floor. "Are you all right?"

"I'm hungry!" Thomasina admitted. "I wish I had eaten last night."

Suddenly, I found myself being picked up and before I knew what was happening I felt the Upright in Trousers smearing something sticky onto my front paws. As I struggled to break free I started to cry out to warn Thomasina. But it was too late. She, I noticed, had already been picked up by the Upright who wears a Skirt.

A moment or two later we sat, side by side, on bare floorboards licking our paws clean.

"Why on earth did they do that?" asked Thomasina, when she had finally managed to remove the last blob of grease.

"It was butter," I explained. "They do it because they think it will help stop us getting lost."

Thomasina looked at me as if I had gone stark, raving mad. "Why on earth should they think that?"

"I think the idea is that by licking the butter off our paws we will pick up the local scent so that when we go out exploring we will be able to find our way back home."

"But we haven't been anywhere yet!" exclaimed Thomasina. "If that's the aim then there is no point in putting butter on our paws until we have been outside."

"I agree!" I said. "But I suppose they're frightened to let us go outside *before* they put the butter on in case we get lost."

Thomasina sighed and shook her head, and I must say that I sympathised with her. Sometimes, even though their intentions might be sensible, Uprights behave as though they really are stupid. The truth is that we cats are much better at finding our way around than Uprights give us credit for. We are not likely to get lost – even if the surroundings are entirely new and unfamiliar.

I was feeling irritated and tired, as well as hungry, and I started to make some untypically abrasive remark about Uprights (for whom I generally have an almost inexhaustible supply of affection) when I heard a lorry arriving outside. I started to move behind my now empty basket, the only object in the room big enough to hide behind, but before I could move more than a couple of feet I found myself being lifted up into the air by the Upright in Trousers. Out of the corner of my eye I saw that the Upright who wears a Skirt had lifted Thomasina up too.

We were carried along a lengthy, bare corridor, up an uncarpeted staircase and unceremoniously dumped in a large room which was dominated by a massive white bath. The bath stood on a plinth in the centre of the room. The house was much larger than the one we had left and there were a hundred fascinating smells to be explored, but Thomasina and I seemed to be doomed to spend all our time in bathrooms.

Ten minutes later, when the Upright who wears a Skirt returned with a large plateful of food, a bowl full of water and the litter tray, we both knew that we were going to be there for some time.

January 3rd

Neither Thomasina nor I slept very well last night. To begin with, we were both kept awake by banging and scraping and bumping and lots of shouting. Then, when the noises finally died away, we were kept awake by our own insatiable sense of curiosity.

I don't think either of us was really *worried* – though we didn't like being shut up in the bathroom one little bit. We were, however, extremely confused, totally bewildered and desperate to know what was happening. We were not really frightened because we trusted our Uprights and knew that they would not let any harm come to us. But we didn't know what was going on, and for a cat there is nothing worse than that. Had we moved home? If so what was our new home like? Would there be good hunting grounds? Was there a garden?

I know a lot of cats are very happy to live indoors and use a litter tray, but I've always had a garden and I think I would miss the opportunity to run around and catch things if I didn't have one.

These questions, and a hundred others, all remained unanswered. But they kept both of us awake for most of the night.

January 4th

The house is wonderful!

It has two staircases and twice as many rooms as our previous home. It is old and dusty, and the skirting boards are full of holes. I have already found two places where it is possible to get right underneath the floorboards. It is full of exciting smells and cupboards and window seats and glorious hiding places.

Outside, the garden stretches for ever and there is a barn, a chicken run and a fine collection of tumble-down sheds and the biggest lavatory you ever saw in your life. The barn has a loft that is absolutely teeming with strange smells and lively mice, and there is a wood and a stream at the bottom of the garden.

"The house is old and dusty and the skirting boards are full of holes."

The kitchen is warm and comfortable and cosy and full of nooks and crannies, and there are two trees within fifty yards of the back door. There is a stable and a tack room that have more exiting smells in them than I ever knew existed, and there are huge spaces on both sides of the refrigerator so that Thomasina and I can catch anything that tries to hide behind it. There is a log shed and a coal shed and a pond and three garden seats and a sundial and goodness knows how many spiders and voles and moles and shrews and lots of things I have never seen before and I am so happy that I think I am about to burst.

January 5th

Today I caught four mice, a vole and two shrews! Thomasina caught three mice and two voles.

January 7th

I woke up feeling very ill and spent the day asleep on the bed. I think I ate too much yesterday.

January 16th

We have been living in our new home for several days now but Thomasina and I are still very excited. We have both spent hours and hours exploring. Judging by the amount of wildlife running about in the house and the outbuildings I don't think there have been any cats living around here for some time. Heaven knows what it's going to be like when spring comes and the animals that have been asleep for the winter start waking up. I doubt if there will be room for us all!

Thomasina says that our new home used to be a farm, and judging by the amount of rusty old machinery lying around in the barn, and the bales of straw still lying in the stable and the tack room, I am sure that she is right.

There are no other houses or even buildings visible from the house, but Thomasina says that she heard a dog barking one morning and since there are no dogs around the house (thank heavens!) that means that there must be another building somewhere in the area.

We have been so busy exploring and hunting that I haven't yet had time to write much in my diary. But I will try to get back into the habit of filling it in properly soon.

January 21st

Today Thomasina caught two mice and very nearly caught a huge black and white bird that looked big enough to know better. I caught a mouse and two shrews.

January 29th

For three days now the house has been swarming with strange Uprights wearing white overalls and carrying ladders and brushes and tins of paint.

I know our Uprights must have invited the strangers into the house, but even they don't seem to enjoy their company very much, and the Upright in Trousers has been in a terrible mood since they arrived.

February 3rd

The Uprights in Overalls are still here.

This morning I thought I had found a quiet place to sleep when I padded into the spare bedroom and found it totally deserted. For a short while I even managed to escape from the terrible smell which has taken over most of the house and ruined any chances Thomasina and I have of doing any serious indoor hunting.

However, I was just enjoying a beautiful dream in which I outwitted the plumpest mouse I had ever dreamt about, when two men burst noisily into the room. One was carrying a ladder and the other had an armful of large, white sheets which he carelessly threw over the bed and the other furniture. For a moment or two I was confused, thinking that perhaps they had come to rescue the mouse, but as soon as I realised what was really happening I darted out between their legs and raced downstairs.

Whenever things seem worrying I always try to get up as high off the ground as I can. No one ever taught me to do this – it's just something that has come naturally.

When I saw a small stepladder near to the back door I instinctively ran to the top of it. From there it was an easy leap onto the top of the oil tank, and from the top of the oil tank I leapt up onto the roof over the back porch.

On reflection I know that I should have been satisfied to be on the roof, but not even *I* always react entirely sensibly and rationally, and I'm afraid that in my desperate panic to escape from the two men who had so rudely interrupted my dream I continued to head upwards.

From the lobby roof I managed to jump up onto the lower reaches of the main roof and I then just carried on heading upwards as far as I could climb.

Eventually, I found myself at the base of a small brick chimney stack. I jumped up onto the top of it without hesitating. It was very sooty and rather smelly, but there was just enough room for me to lie down and make myself fairly comfortable so that is exactly what I did.

"I found myself on a small brick chimney stack. There was just enough room for me to lie down."

That was when I first looked down and realised with some horror just how high up I had climbed.

Everything seemed a long, long, way away, and I suddenly felt very lonely and just a little bit afraid. When I saw that there were birds flying around underneath me I very nearly fainted.

I don't know how long I was up there before anyone noticed that I was missing, but by the time I eventually heard the Uprights whistling and shouting my name I was stiff with fear and didn't dare move so much as a whisker in case I fell. I tried to miaow to let them know where I was but all I could produce was a rather feeble, faint little sound that would have embarrassed a kitten with laryngitis.

Fortunately, Thomasina, who was looking for me in the shrubbery, heard my feeble cries and looked up straight away. Pausing only to let me know that she had seen me she rushed off round to the back of the house, rubbed herself against the legs of the Upright in Trousers and then, when she had got his attention, jumped up on the step ladder and up onto the oil tank. Having made sure that the Upright was watching she looked up at me and miaowed loudly.

The Upright in Trousers was very brave and he scrambled up onto the lobby roof to try and help me down, but he couldn't climb any higher and I couldn't move at all. Eventually I had to submit to the indignity of being rescued by one of the Uprights in Overalls. When he climbed up beside me and put his hands round me my first instinct was to scratch him and run away but there was nowhere to run to, and my fear of falling was far greater than my fear of being picked up. So I did absolutely nothing and allowed him to carry me back down a ladder to the lobby roof. I recovered a final shred of dignity by leaping out of his arms just as he was about to step down onto the top of the oil tank.

I was still shaking twenty minutes later as I lapped at a dish of custard that the Upright who wears a Skirt had given me.

"It was a good job the painters were here!" I heard the Upright in Trousers say. "Without them I don't know how we would have got Alice down."

Sometimes, Uprights say the silliest things. If the Upright in Overalls had not been around I wouldn't have gone up onto the roof in the first place, I would not have got stuck and I would not have needed to be rescued.

What a humiliating day.

Still, there was a golden lining: the custard was lovely.

February 6th

Thomasina and I were in the garden this evening when we heard the Upright in Trousers whistling.

We both knew that he was whistling to tell us that our supper was ready but we decided not to take any notice of him.

"I'm fed up of being expected to respond to a whistle," complained Thomasina. "It's rude!"

I agreed with Thomasina, and we decided that in future we would only respond if the Upright called us by our names.

February 8th

There is a door in the downstairs hall which is normally kept closed.

But this morning one of the Uprights failed to shut it properly and so Thomasina and I poked our heads through the gap to see what there was on the other side.

It was very dark, and at first we couldn't see anything. But slowly our eyes got accustomed to the lack of light and, to our absolute astonishment, we discovered that the house has another staircase!

Tentatively, we edged forwards. Then, slowly, we walked down two short flights of wooden stairs.

At first we thought that the stairs were just "spares" – kept there in case either of the house's other two staircases needed replacing. (The Uprights are very keen on having plenty of "spares" – they have far more clothes and cups and saucers than they could possibly ever need).

But then we discovered that at the bottom of the stairs, underneath the rest of the house, there are several brick walled, stone floored, secret rooms.

I do not think I have ever seen anything quite so exciting.

The underground rooms were piled high with stout cardboard boxes, large wooden chests, dusty suitcases and old bits of forgotten and abandoned furniture.

There was a cupboard with one door missing, two chairs with only six legs between them and a standard lamp with no shade. There were boxes full of books, toys, crockery and saucepans. There were old kettles, old electric fires and, in one corner, a huge pile of coal!

But it was, inevitably, the wildlife which Thomasina and I found most exciting.

We could smell mice galore and Thomasina said she was sure that there had been a rat or two down there in the not too distant past. Spiders scuttled off into the shadows as we explored, and dozens of huge, silken, motionless webs, studded with the decaying corpses of dead flies, decorated the walls and the ceilings.

I don't know how long Thomasina and I spent down there, but our hunting attempts were not as successful as we had hoped they would be and eventually, tired, dusty and hungry we decided to climb back up the stairs to see if it was time to get something to eat from the Uprights.

When we got back to the top of the staircase we found, to our horror, that the door out into the hall had been closed and bolted on the other side. We were locked in!

For several hours we took it in turns to scratch at the door and to miaow for help. By the time the Upright who wears a Skirt heard us and let us out we were both exhausted and very hungry.

I do not think we will be going through that door and down those stairs again in a hurry.

It may have been exciting in those secret, hidden rooms but neither Thomasina nor I fancy the idea of getting locked in again.

February 14th

An hour or so after the Uprights had gone out this evening I heard a terrible noise coming from the bathroom. When I went upstairs to see what was happening I discovered that the noise was coming from inside the bath itself.

I jumped up onto the wooden stool that the Uprights keep at the bottom of the bath and found that it was Thomasina who was making all the noise. She was racing round and round in circles, apparently intent on catching her own tail.

"What on earth are you doing?"

Thomasina stopped the moment she heard me and looked up. I could see that she was extremely embarrassed.

"How long have you been there?" she demanded.

"Oh, just a few moments."

"You shouldn't spy. It isn't very nice."

"I've never been tempted to chase my tail. I know exactly where it is and I'm happy to leave it there unmolested."

"I wasn't spying!" I protested. "I heard the noise and came to see what it was." I paused. "Anyway, what were you doing?"

"I was chasing my tail," said Thomasina defiantly. She stared up at me for a moment. "Why shouldn't I?"

I was genuinely puzzled. "But *why*?" I asked.

I have never been tempted to chase my tail. I know exactly where it is and I'm very happy to leave it there, unmolested.

Thomasina shrugged and then jumped up onto the rim of the bath. "Because it's there!"

"Do you ever catch it?"

"No!" admitted Thomasina, jumping down onto the floor. "That's half the fun." And with that she stalked off out of the bathroom, with both her tail and her head held high.

February 17th

"It's good practice, you know!"

I opened an eye and looked up. Thomasina was sitting on the arm of the sofa staring down at me.

"What is?"

"Chasing my tail."

For a moment or two I didn't know what she was talking about. Then I remembered. Thomasina was clearly still embarrassed about my catching her in the bath a few nights ago.

"Oh, good," I said.

"It helps to keep me in shape."

"That's nice."

"It does!"

"I believe you!" I insisted, closing my eye again. "Now, do you mind if I go back to sleep?"

I didn't say anything else because I would not hurt Thomasina for the world, but I can't see how chasing your tail in the bath can possibly be good practice for anything apart from chasing your tail in the bath.

Frankly, I am surprised that Thomasina cannot see that.

February 19th

The door that leads to the secret staircase was left open again this morning.

Thomasina and I took it in turns to go down and explore.

While she hunted I stayed at the top of the stairs in case one of the Uprights decided to shut the door. And then she did the same while I did a little hunting.

But although we both saw plenty of mice neither of us caught anything.

February 20th

I do love our Uprights. They are loyal, faithful and affectionate; kindly, generous and always there when we need them.

This morning I woke up feeling miserable. I don't know why. There wasn't any reason for it. But I felt perfectly gloomy and very depressed. It was as though a huge black cloud was hovering overhead and had blocked out all the sunshine.

After breakfast I meandered over to the living room sofa, curled up into a ball and lay there feeling sorry for myself.

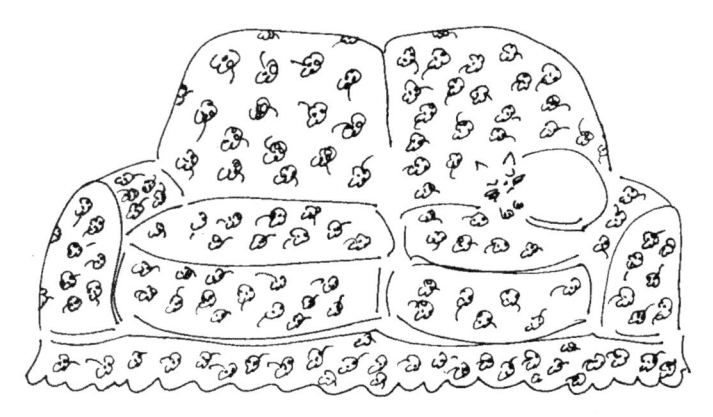

"I meandered over to the living room sofa, curled myself up into a ball and lay there feeling sorry for myself."

Somehow, the Upright who wears a Skirt must have known that I was feeling miserable for she stopped what she was doing in the kitchen and came over to sit beside me. She didn't say anything, but for the best part of half an hour she just stroked my back in that gentle, soothing, rhythmic way she has. When she finally stopped she lowered her head and gave me a kiss before getting up and going back to her chores in the kitchen.

I don't know whether the Upright who wears a Skirt has magic in her fingertips but she certainly has plenty of love in them, and when she left me I felt a million times better. The black cloud had blown away and the sun was shining through again.

I have often argued that Uprights are more intelligent and loving than we give them credit for and I think that this incident justifies my argument.

February 22nd

Today, I caught four mice, two voles and two shrews.

It would have been even more but a third shrew, which I had cornered behind the potting shed, escaped when I lost concentration for a moment and fell asleep.

When I told Thomasina of my hunting successes she was quite offhand. She said it was not polite to boast of one's achievements.

But I was not boasting! I was merely reporting the facts. And what on earth is wrong with that? Are we only supposed to tell others of our mistakes and failures?

Thomasina's attitude quite spoilt the day for me.

February 23rd

I have been thinking a lot about what Thomasina said yesterday. And the more I think about it the more I am convinced that she was quite wrong to criticise me in the way she did.

I agree with her that *boasting* can be unpleasant and embarrassing. But I think that simple pride can be more of a virtue than a sin.

We should, I think, all have pride in our skills and achievements. Pride gives us courage and determination and enables us to achieve more. Pride is only a sin when it leads to arrogance, vanity and a contempt for others.

February 28th

The Uprights had visitors today and they brought a small, noisy dog with them. Halfway through the afternoon one of the Visiting Uprights pulled a paper bag out of his pocket and took out a handful of small, bone shaped biscuits. What followed was probably one of the most embarrassing and humiliating things I have ever seen in my life.

The Visiting Upright held one of the biscuits up in the air a foot or so above the dog's nose. And the dog sat back on his haunches and *begged* for it!

All the Uprights seemed to think that this was very clever – as though begging was a special trick that had to be learned.

But Thomasina and I were so disgusted that we left the room and refused to go back into the house until the dog had left.

I would, I think, rather starve to death than beg for food. Whatever happened to dignity and self respect?

March 2nd

For several minutes I could not work out where I was or what had happened to me.

Wherever I was it was pitch black and although I was curled up on a long roll of comfortable carpet everything around me seemed to be rattling and shaking. I could smell paint and petrol, and a few inches from my nose a couple of cans filled with tin tacks were sliding and shuffling and scraping about on a metal floor.

Above my head a metal ladder was hanging from two protruding metal brackets and every few seconds it swung closer and closer to the edge of the brackets; occasionally it banged noisily against a metal wall.

Gingerly, I clambered to my feet. It was not easy to stay upright because the floor on which I was standing kept moving about. Three of the metal walls which surrounded me were solid; the fourth, which was divided into two halves, had what looked like a handle in the middle of it and two panes of glass set into the upper parts of each half. Through these two windows I could see a constantly changing pattern of bright lights.

At long last I remembered what had happened.

It had been a beautiful spring day; sunny but quite cool, and I had decided to spend it asleep on the window seat in the Uprights' bedroom. After half an hour or so my peace had been rudely shattered by the sound of banging.

A moment or two later I discovered that two strange Uprights were hammering a new carpet into position on the front staircase.

Without waiting for them to find me I ran out along the top landing, down the back stairs, through the kitchen and out through the cat flap in the back door to safety. I do so hate it when our Uprights allow strangers to come into the house.

Outside, although it was beautifully sunny, it was noticeably cooler than it had looked from the comfort of the bedroom window seat and I decided to look around for somewhere warm where I could curl up and continue my sleep. I had been enjoying a particularly pleasant dream in which Thomasina and I had been chasing a whole family of succulent field mice and I was eager to resume my imaginary adventures.

It was, I suspect, this urge to return to my dream which led me to leap up into the back of a van parked outside the back door and to curl up in a dark, but cosy, hollow between two rolls of carpet. The van doors had been left wide open and it never occurred to me that I would ever find myself trapped inside the vehicle when it was driven away.

But that is exactly what happened.

When I eventually realised that as each minute went by I was being driven further and further away from my home I began to feel very lonely, very frightened and very unhappy. I paced about unsteadily inside the back of the van, occasionally looking out of the rear windows and all the time struggling to keep my footing. I wondered if I would ever again see Thomasina, my Uprights or the beautiful new house I was growing to love so much.

I don't know how far the van travelled after I had woken up but the journey seemed to take a lifetime. By the time the driver eventually stopped I felt physically exhausted and mentally drained. Shaking with fear, and terrified about what I would find waiting for me outside the van, I waited for the back door to open. When, at last, it did I leapt down past the outstretched hand of a startled Upright who attempted to stop me, and out into a world about which I knew absolutely nothing.

The Carpet Fitting Uprights had parked their van in a small yard alongside several other similar vehicles, and my dash for freedom took me through a gate, over a brick wall and across a dimly lit street which was far busier with traffic than any thoroughfare I had ever seen before.

After I had run as fast as I could for five minutes or so I crawled behind a row of metal dustbins to get my breath back. I could feel my heart beating furiously inside my chest and my whole body felt uncomfortably alive with fear and expectation.

I had no idea how far the van had come or where I was.

I had not intended to stay where I was for more than a few moments but when I did try to move I found that my legs just didn't want to work.

Feeling unhappier than I had ever felt before I made myself as comfortable as I could and tried to go to sleep.

March 3rd

I was woken up by a deafening noise.

When I looked up I saw that one of the nearby dustbins had been tipped right over onto its side. Three cats were speedily picking their way through the rubbish and pouncing eagerly on anything that looked edible.

At first I thought that they would be too busy to notice me, but all cats can sense the presence of other animals and these were alert, street wise, city cats.

"Hello, Splodge!" said one of them, pulling the remains of a beefburger out of a discarded bun. He was jet black, but even so I could tell that his fur was horribly dirty. He was looking directly at me as he spoke but I looked around to make sure that there was no one behind me.

"I'm talking to you!" said the black cat. "Splodge!"

He laughed. "I've never seen so many colours on one cat." He turned towards his two companions and grinned.

"My name is Alice," I said, quietly but firmly.

The other two cats, who had been fighting over a small piece of fish, broke off to stare at me. One of them was light grey and had a white patch around his left eye which gave him a distinctly piratical air. The other, a mackerel tabby, had very similar markings to Thomasina.

"My name is Alice," mimicked the light grey cat cruelly.

"What are you doing here?" demanded the mackerel tabby.

"A nearby dustbin had been tipped onto its side and three cats were picking their way through the rubbish."

I started to explain, but the black cat didn't want an explanation. "This is our territory!" he snapped. "Go away and find your own dustbins."

I tried to tell him that all I wanted to do was to go home to Thomasina and my Uprights but he was not interested. Without any warning he leapt forwards and, with astonishing speed, clawed the left hand side of my face. He was so fast, and the attack was so completely unprovoked and unexpected, that I failed to get out of the way. A moment or two later I felt something warm and sticky trickling into the corner of my left eye. Blood.

If the black cat had been alone I might have been tempted to stay and fight, but I knew that with three of them I had no chance of winning so I turned and ran away as quickly as I could. As I ran I could hear the three alley cats behind me laughing and making rude remarks. Although I pretended to myself that I didn't care I felt lonelier and more afraid than at any time since I had arrived in the city.

I was still running at full speed when I turned a corner and almost collided head on with the largest cat I have ever seen in my life. He was ginger, and from the scars he bore it was clear that he was an experienced street fighter.

"Whoa! Not so fast!" said the ginger cat, holding out a paw to stop me. "What's the hurry?"

"I'm sorry," I apologised, slightly breathless from all the running I had done. I've always been proud of my good health and fitness but nothing I had ever experienced had prepared me for city life. "I came here in a carpet van by mistake and now I want to go home. Three cats I met thought I was trying to steal food from their dustbins but I wasn't." The words came tumbling out in a great rush.

The ginger cat laughed. "Have you had any breakfast?"

I shook my head, suddenly realising how hungry I was.

"Would you like some?"

After a moment's hesitation I nodded furiously.

"Then you'd better tell me all about it over breakfast," said the ginger cat kindly. Even when he wasn't laughing the ginger cat had a friendly twinkle in his eyes. "My name is Ginger," he told me. "What's yours?"

I told him.

"That's a nice name," he said, and I think he meant it.

Fifteen minutes later, after we had finished a breakfast of raw fish heads (which I enjoyed far more than I thought I would, though to be honest I was so hungry that I would have probably enjoyed a meal of cardboard plates) I told Ginger my story.

"I felt tears streaming down my face."

He sat still for a few moments after I had finished, then licked a small piece of fish from the corner of his mouth. "What a silly young cat you are!" He shook his head and then leant forwards. "You should never, ever get into a strange vehicle – however great the temptation."

"I realise that now," I said, rather tearfully. "I've learned my lesson. All I want to do now is to go home."

"Do you know where Thomasina and your Uprights live?"

I nodded. "Over there!" I said, indicating a distant spot somewhere over his left shoulder.

Ginger half turned to stare in the direction of the derelict building towards which I had nodded. "I'm sure you know which direction to take," he sighed. "All cats have a perfect sense of direction. But do you know how far you've got to travel? And do you know how you're going to get there?"

Feeling downcast I lowered my eyes. "I'm going to walk," I muttered defiantly. "I don't care how far it is."

"Good!" said Ginger. "You're going to need all the determination you can muster." He paused and looked carefully at me. "Have you ever lived in a city before?"

I hesitated for a moment but then shook my head firmly. I wanted to tell Ginger the truth.

Ginger sighed loudly. "You don't know how to scrounge without annoying other cats? You don't know how to survive the traffic, the dogs, the kids and the catnappers?"

"No," I said in a tiny little voice that seemed to come from a long way away. I had no idea that there were so many hazards in the city. I felt further from home than ever before. All I had left were my memories of the past and my hopes for the future.

I felt tears streaming down my cheeks and hurriedly wiped them away with a grubby paw. For the first time I wondered if I would ever find my way home again.

"Don't worry!" said Ginger. "I'll teach you – but it'll take a few days. If you try to leave now you'll never get out of here alive."

March 6th

"I'll never be able to fight like you," I told Ginger, after I had watched him scare off two alley cats who had tried to steal our evening meal from us.

"You don't have to be able to fight," said Ginger. "Just be prepared to run at the first sight of trouble."

"But isn't running away cowardly?"

"No!" said Ginger emphatically. "Running away is sensible." He stopped for a moment and thought. "There's only one thing more sensible than running," he added. "And that is not being there at all when there is trouble around."

"But how . . .?"

"Learn to judge potentially difficult or dangerous situations well in advance," Ginger told me. "Keep away from groups of dustbins where there are bound to be lots of cats, avoid school playgrounds and always cross over the road when you see a dog or hear one barking."

Not for the first time Ginger reminded me of another wise cat I once knew called George. I wished that they could have met for I think they would have enjoyed one another's company.

March 9th

Something that happened today made me realise just how dangerous life in the city can be.

For several days now Ginger has been teaching me a basic survival course and the single most important thing I have learned is that whenever possible sensible cats keep away from ground level.

"You will probably have to come down to eat," Ginger explained. "But try to spend as much time as you can on rooftops. Always travel across rooftops and always, always sleep on rooftops."

I must have looked doubtful. I have never been very good on roofs, and I couldn't help remembering that just a short while ago I had been stuck on the roof of our own house.

"There are no dogs or children up here," explained Ginger as we sat together on a flat roof above a garage. "And there's no chance ...". Suddenly, he stopped talking and pointed down to the street below us. I followed his extended paw with my eyes and watched as two Uprights jumped out of a small, dark, blue van.

"What is it?"

"Sssshhhh!" hissed Ginger. "Just watch!"

The two Uprights opened the back of their van and took out a large net. They put on thick leather gloves and then they advanced stealthily towards a large pile of rubbish that lay blocking a nearby alleyway. Moving quickly and silently the two Uprights leapt onto the top of the plastic bags and cardboard boxes and threw their net over two cats who tried, too late, to make a run for it. One of the cats was, I realised, the grey cat with the piratical eye patch who had helped to chase me away from my first hiding place.

With the two cats struggling in their net the Uprights, now laughing and joking together, walked back across the street to their van. They removed the cats from the netting and put them into small wire cages. Then they put the cages into the van, tossed the net on top of them, slammed the doors and drove off.

"Why did they do that?" I asked, horrified.

"They're catnappers," explained Gingerly simply.

I was puzzled. "But why? What are they going to do with those two cats?"

"Sell them to Uprights in White Coats," explained Ginger.

"The two Uprights put on thick leather gloves."

I didn't understand. I know that many Uprights enjoy the company of cats but I found Ginger's claim difficult to believe. My doubts must have showed.

"They use the cats for experiments," said Ginger quietly. "They do the experiments while the cats are still alive."

"What sort of experiments?"

Ginger shrugged. "All sorts of things. I've heard that they blind them and poison them. Sometimes they just chop bits out of them.'

"And the cats are alive when these terrible things are done to them?"

"Oh yes."

"But why do the Uprights in White Coats do it? What's the point of it?"

"Some say they experiment on cats so that they can find out what will happen if the same things happen to Uprights," said Ginger.

I must have looked as puzzled as I felt.

"They try out new drugs and new operations on cats before trying them on Uprights," explained Ginger.

"But that's crazy! How could Uprights learn anything useful by doing experiments on *us*? I wouldn't want to take a drug that had been tried out on Uprights! They are completely different to us."

"I agree with you," sighed Ginger, with a shrug. "Deep down I think they just do the experiments because they like doing them."

I shuddered. I had never realised that any Uprights could be so cruel. But I had learned an important lesson. As long as I remained in the city I would follow Ginger's advice and stay on the rooftops as much as possible. I didn't want the catnappers to get me.

March 11th

Ginger has taught me how to survive, how to find food, how to find good, safe sleeping places and how to avoid some of the worst dangers of city life.

Today, when I woke up, I knew that it was time for me to leave his care and start making my way home.

"Are you sure that you're ready?" asked Ginger. "This is a big city. I've never been out to the edge of it myself."

"I don't think I'll ever *really* be ready," I confessed. "But I have to get home. I know that Thomasina and my Uprights will be worried about me." I paused and could feel my throat constricting. "And I miss them all terribly," I added quietly. "I miss them all so very much."

Ginger nodded wisely. "Just remember what I told you. Travel across the roofs as much as you can, and if you see anything that looks like potential trouble steer well clear of it."

"Travel across the roofs as much as you can"

"I will!" I promised him.

I knew that I had to say "goodbye" and I knew that I was going to miss Ginger. He had taught me how to stay alive, but more than that, he had given me strength and companionship and he had helped restore my faith in myself and in the world. When I had first met him I had felt more alone, more desperate and more unhappy than at any previous moment in my life.

How could I ever thank him for everything he had done for me?

"Goodbye!" I said. "And, thank you." It sounded bald and nowhere near enough.

"Goodbye!" said Ginger. "And good luck!" Somehow, in a strange way that I couldn't easily explain, I felt that he would probably miss me as much as I knew I would miss him.

March 14th

Today was, I think, one of the saddest and most depressing days of my life.

My route back home took me south, and this morning I found myself passing the carpet warehouse where I had jumped out of the Uprights' van not so very long ago.

My heart was beating twice as fast as usual as I kept low and tried to pass by unnoticed when I suddenly heard a voice that I instantly recognised.

It was the Upright in Trousers!

I looked through the wire mesh fencing that surrounded the warehouse and the parking area and I could see him standing about a hundred yards away, talking to another Upright who wore dark blue overalls. The stranger, whom I had never seen before, was shaking his head. The two of them were standing in what was clearly a parking area for vans and cars.

Desperate, I cried out as loudly as I could and tried to climb up the fence which separated us. But the sound of car engines drowned my cries and the fence was impossible to climb. Frustrated, I tried to will him to look in my direction. But that didn't work either.

"I looked through the wire-mesh fencing."

Moments later the Upright in Trousers, who looked ravaged by sadness and dispirited and depressed, climbed back into his motor car and drove away. He had, I knew, been looking for me.

But I didn't give up!

I ran alongside the fence until I found the entrance to the warehouse and then I ran through the gate, hoping that the Upright in Trousers would have left a description of me with the Upright in Blue Overalls.

But I never found out if he had.

Before I could find the Upright in Blue Overalls two younger Uprights spotted me and started to throw small stones at me. I tried to dodge them but they were good shots and they hit me several times. In despair and pain, and with my eyes filled with tears, I turned round and ran out of the warehouse car park.

I was, I realised, going to have to find my own way home.

March 16th

Last night I dreamt that I was back home.

I dreamt that I ate a plateful of chicken and a bowl of custard and then went to sleep in front of a blazing log fire with Thomasina beside me.

The Upright in Trousers and the Upright who wears a Skirt were sitting with us watching the television.

But when I woke up I was cold and hungry and suffering from cramp. Thomasina wasn't there and nor were the Uprights. I felt very sad.

March 18th

A bag of chips saved my life this evening.

I had not eaten for two days and I was beginning to feel weak with hunger when suddenly my nose began to twitch: I could smell something hot and tasty.

"I dreamt that I went to sleep in front of a blazing log fire with Thomasina beside me."

The chips had been dropped on the pavement and the bag had burst. Greedily, I ate them up as fast as I could before the smell attracted any other cats.

March 19th

I slept badly and was woken up several times by terrible indigestion.

March 22nd

If I had been able to walk home in a straight line and without having to stop to find food or to sleep I would have probably been there by now.

But every day my journey is complicated and lengthened by the need to find something to eat and somewhere safe to sleep.

In addition, remembering Ginger's advice, I often make lengthy detours in order to avoid potentially dangerous areas.

For example, I always keep well away when I hear the sounds of children playing in a school-yard, and if I can't avoid crossing busy roads I try to cross them at night.

My searches for food take up much of my time. I have always been used to being able to catch plenty of fresh meat but here in the city there are more rats than mice and far more dogs than shrews or voles. In the time when I should be finding food to eat I seem to waste hours avoiding being eaten!

Today, for example, all I've eaten is a puddle of oil I found underneath an old car. It tasted horrible and very nearly made me sick but I ate it because I remember my dear old friend George telling me that, as a last resort, oil can help to keep a cat alive.

He told me about a cat called Emily who was accidentally nailed into a crate in Detroit in America along with a diesel engine which was being shipped to Cairo. The journey lasted for 41 days and Emily had no food or water but, when the crate was opened she, and the four kittens she had given birth to on the journey, were all alive. They had survived by licking the oil from the engine.

After I had finished licking up the oil I felt so tired and sick that I just wanted to lie down and go to sleep. I had covered a considerable distance and thought I had earned a rest. It was already getting dark and the night was star-less, cold and miserable.

Mindful of Ginger's advice always to find somewhere safe to sleep, and conscious of the need to find somewhere high up (away from dogs, motor cars and catnappers), I jumped up onto a low wall, slithered

"All I'd eaten was a puddle of oil I found underneath an old car."

across a sloping roof and climbed up and up until I could go no further. As I went I couldn't help thinking how much better I had become at dealing with heights.

Suddenly, to my absolute astonishment, I smelt soft damp earth, fresh grass and sweetly scented flowers. At first I thought that my senses must have deceived me but they had not. Right up high, where normally I would have expected to find nothing but chimney pots and roof tiles, I had found a secret piece of hidden countryside.

Delighted by my discovery I dug a proper earth lavatory for the first time in days, ate a few blades of grass to help settle my stomach and snuggled down for the night underneath a small, exquisitely perfumed lavender bush.

March 23rd

I woke with a start this morning, distinctly conscious that someone was staring at me. Cautiously, I raised an eyelid and looked around without moving my head.

A young, nervous looking siamese cat was standing about six feet away. For a few moments neither of us said anything.

"Am I trespassing?" I asked at last.

One of the important things I have learned in the city is that cats who live here are very jealous of their territories – in my admittedly limited experience, far more so than cats who live in suburban or country areas. I am also aware that the peculiar and sometimes disgusting smells which fill city streets often make it difficult to tell where one cat's territory starts and another ends.

The siamese just looked rather startled but did not reply. I looked around. I seemed to be in a garden. But I knew I was on a rooftop. I was puzzled and said so.

"It's a roof garden," explained the siamese cat.

"Who does it belong to?"

"My Uprights," explained the siamese cat. "They own the penthouse flat and the garden comes with it."

"Is this real earth?"

She nodded.

"Real grass?"

"Yes."

"Real flowers?"

Another nod.

"How did they get it all up here?"

The siamese cat looked puzzled at this last question, as though it indicated a train of thought that had never troubled her before.

"I don't know," she admitted.

Mentally I shrugged. I know enough about Uprights to realise that not everything they do is explicable.

"Are you hungry?" asked the siamese cat.

I was. I said so.

The siamese disappeared for a few moments and came back a little later dragging a large piece of chicken breast with her. It was so large that she had to walk with her forelegs either side of it. She dropped it a few inches in front of me and then backed away.

"Don't you want any?"

She shook her head. "I've eaten."

Without any further hesitation I started to tear into the chicken. It was, I thought, one of the tastiest meals I had ever eaten. It was marvellous. I didn't stop until I had finished.

"You *were* hungry!" exclaimed the siamese cat. She was not being rude, just honest. I don't think she had ever before seen a cat so hungry.

"That was lovely!" I told her. "Thank you!"

"What's your name?"

"Alice. What's yours?"

"Princess Samantha. But my Uprights call me Smokey."

"That's nice."

"Are you lost?"

"Not really." I explained that although I had found her Uprights garden by mistake I was not really properly lost but was on my way back home. I told her what had happened to me.

"How terrible!" said Smokey, genuinely sympathetic. Slowly, a frown appeared on her face. "But how on earth do you know which way to go? I'm sure I would get completely and utterly lost if I found myself outside the garden."

"You wouldn't!" I assured her. "You've got a compass in your head that would help you find your way home wherever you were."

"I have?" She sounded sceptical.

"All cats have," I insisted.

Smokey still didn't seem very convinced so I told her about Toby who walked 300 miles in four months to get from Cornwall to Kent; Marshall who covered 120 miles in six weeks to get from London to Lowestoft and a cat called, like her, Smokey who covered 285

"I seemed to be in a garden. But I knew I was on a rooftop."

miles to travel from Newquay in Cornwall to Bexhill in Sussex and did it in just three months.

"That's extraordinary!" said Smokey, sounding genuinely impressed and more than a little excited. "And you think I could do it if I had to?"

"Of course you could!" I assured her. And I told her about a cat called Libby who, when she was just two years old was sent by her Uprights, who lived in Chichester, to stay with an elderly Upright, who lived in Brighton.

"Libby was very happy there," I said. "But after a year her new Upright died. So what do you think she did?"

Smokey looked at me with eyes wide open. "I don't know," she murmured breathlessly. "What did she do?"

"She walked back to Chichester!" I told her triumphantly. "Twenty five miles in just over one week."

Smokey seemed impressed, but her thirst for knowledge was still not quenched. "If I was doing this would I just travel in a straight line?"

"More or less. But you'd have to find bridges over rivers and canals. And crossing busy roads can be dangerous so you wouldn't want to do that too often."

"How wonderful!" purred Smokey. She put her head on one side and smiled. "We cats are marvellous, aren't we?"

I had to smile as I nodded.

I stayed with Smokey for the whole of the day, resting and getting my strength back. From a corner of her Uprights' roof garden I could see green fields, but although I knew that my journey through the city was almost over I knew that I still had a long way to go before I arrived back home.

In the evening Smokey brought me a large piece of fresh fish that she said was called salmon. Normally, I hate fish and I certainly didn't like it as much as the chicken, but it tasted much better than engine oil and I was very grateful to her.

"You have some!" I begged, stopping for a moment, and feeling guilty at the haste with which I had been eating.

"No! Really!" insisted Smokey. "My Uprights are very good to me. I'll go and get them to give me something else a little later."

Those were by far the two best meals I had eaten since I had been away from home.

As I settled down to go to sleep I felt very homesick. I couldn't help thinking about Thomasina and my own Uprights. In a way I felt that they were probably worse off than I am. They will, I know, be terribly worried about me. At least I know that I am still alive and well. And I know that I am on my way home. They can only hope and pray.

March 26th

Early this morning I cut my right front paw. I didn't realise I had done it until I felt my paw sticking uncomfortably to the pavement as I plodded on towards home. I stopped straight away and licked it clean but the wound looked quite deep. I suspect that I must have trodden on a piece of glass. I do hope that it doesn't become infected.

March 29th

My right front paw is very sore and swollen today. I know that I should probably stop and rest until it gets better but I want to get home as quickly as possible so I am going to carry on.

April 2nd

I have found that by half hopping and half skipping I can make quite good progress and can move a little faster than by merely limping along.

April 5th

There are now quite large gaps between the houses and although the traffic is faster than it was in the middle of the city there is much less of it. The air

"My right front paw is very sore and swollen."

smells sweeter, and instead of having to rely on finding food in dustbins I have been able to catch fresh food twice in the last forty eight hours.

My paw is still very sore and it slows me down a lot but fortunately the mice around here seem rather fat and lazy.

April 8th

When I woke this morning I wasted three hours walking in completely the wrong direction. I don't know what came over me – I must have been half asleep.

Instead of walking towards our new home I headed for the house where the Uprights, Thomasina and I all used to live.

"I wasted three hours walking in completely the wrong direction."

April 11th

I have been making much better progress since I left the city behind. Yesterday, I left the road completely and set off across the fields. It is now over twenty four hours since I saw a house or an Upright.

The only scary moment came late last night when, while hobbling through a small area of woodland, I came face to face with a fox. I don't know which one of us was most startled but I reacted first and scrambled high up into an old oak tree. I spent the night up the tree and felt very safe.

April 14th

My paw is now very swollen and so tender that I have to hold it out of the way while I am trying to walk. If I knock it on anything it hurts a lot.

Nevertheless, I managed to catch a mouse and a shrew today. I am so glad that I spent some time learning to hunt. If I had not been able to catch my own food I hate to think what would have happened to me by now. I suspect that I would have been unable to leave the city at all!

April 15th

The countryside is beautiful. I love the fields, the trees, the flowers and the fresh country air. Why do so many Uprights live in towns and cities? Are they all being punished for something they have done wrong?

April 18th

Ever since I found myself in the back of the carpet van, miles from home, I have frequently dreamt of

"I spent the night up a tree and felt very safe."

the moment when I would arrive back with Thomasina and my Uprights.

In my dream I arrived home on a warm, sunny day. I saw myself gazing down at our house from the top of a nearby hill and breathing a deep sigh of relief as I realised that I had got back safely.

In my dream I always had time to savour the sweet moment of my home coming.

But it didn't happen quite like that.

When I woke up this morning I set off through a meadow of tall grass thinking that I had a journey of several days length ahead of me. My inbuilt compass told me that I was travelling in the right direction but it didn't tell me how far I had to travel.

And I kept walking all day. Even after the sun had gone down I still kept limping on. I was physically exhausted, but my desperation to be home gave me reserves of strength I did not know I had.

Suddenly, quite without warning, I found myself standing looking through a simple wooden fence at our new home and garden. There was only half a moon to light the scene but it was a view I will never, ever forget.

The house and the garden were exactly as I remembered them and there, sitting on the front door step was Thomasina. She looked thinner than I remembered her and there was a sad, faraway look in her eyes that I had never seen before.

Finding one last burst of energy I leapt up onto the top of the wooden fence and then jumped down into the garden.

The sound of my landing attracted Thomasina's attention and, suddenly alert, she looked across in my direction. For a moment I don't think she recognised me but then, when she realised who it was, she gave out a squeal of delight and hurled herself across the lawn towards me. Moments later she was licking my face and purring louder than I have ever heard a cat purr before. I felt so happy that I thought I would burst.

I was home!

If I live to be 100 years old I doubt if I will ever experience a more complete moment of happiness.

After Thomasina and I had greeted one another

and had licked the sadness and the tears from one another's faces we both instinctively made our way towards the cat flap in the back door so that I could go and say "hello" to the Uprights.

"I set off through a meadow of tall grass."

As I limped along behind Thomasina I remembered every room, every doorway and every piece of furniture with tenderness and affection. As we climbed the darkened stairs to the Uprights' bedroom I remembered the long, frightening days and nights when only the thought of being home again had kept me alive. Each freshly remembered smell and each creak from the floorboards reminded me how much I had missed my home. I vowed that I would never again take any of it for granted.

As we walked together along the landing I could hear the gentle snoring sound the Upright in Trousers makes when he sleeps and, strangely enough, it was that which brought the biggest lump to my throat.

Thomasina was so excited that she couldn't wait. She sprang forward ahead of me, shot through the door into the Uprights' bedroom and leapt up onto the bed, miaowing loudly as she did so. I heard one of the Uprights sit up and switch on the light.

As I followed through the doorway I could see the Upright in Trousers sitting up in bed and rubbing his eyes. I thought for a brief moment that he might have been cross at being awakened so rudely but he was not. He leant forward, rubbed his fingers through Thomasina's coat and asked her what the matter was. Then the Upright who wears a Skirt sat up too.

When Thomasina jumped down off the bed and came and sat beside me in the doorway the Upright in Trousers threw back the bed clothes, jumped out of bed, crossed the bedroom floor in an instant and knelt down beside me.

"It's Alice!" he cried, with tears already forming in his eyes. "She's back!"

He picked me up and held me to him, stroking me and saying my name over and over again. As he held me he accidently and inadvertently pressed on my poorly paw. I tried hard not to show the pain I felt but he noticed immediately that something was wrong and gently lay me down on the bed so that both he and the Upright who wears a Skirt could examine me.

"You poor thing," said the Upright who wears a Skirt, stroking me and kissing my head. I felt something wet fall onto my fur, looked up and saw that tears were pouring down her cheeks.

The next few minutes were a confusing mixture of emotions. The Uprights made me a large bowl of custard which Thomasina insisted I eat all by myself, and then filled a huge plate with pieces of cold chicken which Thomasina did agree to share.

Half an hour or so later the Upright who smells of Antiseptic arrived. He examined my paw gently, and bathed it in some nasty smelling fluid. Then he gave me an injection in my neck. I don't know why he did that because there was nothing wrong with my neck but he was very gentle and kind and I was so glad to be home that I would have let him do almost anything.

When he had gone the Uprights took us both back upstairs and we all went to sleep together; the two Uprights snuggled up to one another underneath the bedclothes and Thomasina and I snuggled together at the foot of the bed.

April 19

I am normally a light sleeper but when I awoke this morning I was alone. A bright shaft of sunlight was cutting like a blade through a tiny gap in the still drawn curtains and faint whispers from a far corner of the house told me that both the Uprights were downstairs. From the distant rattles I guessed that they were having breakfast. I had no idea where Thomasina was.

For a moment or two I completely forgot the horrors I had been through during my adventure in the city. Then, slowly, I became aware of the throbbing pain in my right paw and a series of savage, unpleasant memories flooded back.

Gingerly, I climbed down off the bed and limped along the landing. I felt totally exhausted, as though now that I was home my body had allowed itself to recognise the extent of the tiredness it had for so long been denying. I was so tired that it seemed to take me a lifetime to reach the top of the stairs.

When I finally reached the kitchen I had to sit down in the doorway and rest. The two Uprights saw me at the same moment and both got up from the table and hurried over towards me. They were very kind. The Upright in Trousers stroked my back and tickled me underneath my chin while the Upright who wears a Skirt filled a bowl with creamy milk and put it down right in front of me.

When I had drunk a little milk and rested for a while I continued on my way towards the back door.

"I had to sit down in the doorway and rest."

On my way I noticed that the thoughtful Uprights had put a seed tray filled with earth inside the porch.

For a moment I was tempted but pride won out over exhaustion. Wearily, I hobbled straight for the nearest patch of garden where I found Thomasina waiting for me beside a hole she had obviously just dug.

"I thought you might need a little help," she said, nodding towards the hole to indicate that she had dug it for me. She put her head on one side and smiled at me. I felt full of love for her. What more thoughtful thing could any cat do? Then she turned away and walked off to give me privacy.

A few moments later, as I limped back towards the house Thomasina came up to me with a plump, freshly caught field mouse in her mouth. She dropped the mouse at my feet, stunned it with one blow of her paw and then backed away. I was very touched and although I was not really all that hungry I ate it all up.

It is wonderful to be back home surrounded by so much warmth and love.

April 20th

I spent the whole of the day resting on the window seat in the bedroom.

April 21st

I feel a little stronger today. My paw does not hurt quite so much.

April 24th

I nearly caught a rabbit today. But it got away. I hate rabbits anyway.

April 27th

For two days now the weather has been so hot that neither Thomasina nor I have ventured outside except when absolutely necessary. The paving slabs on the terrace have been too hot for comfort, and even the earth is baking in the heat. Most of our energy has been spent on trying to find cool places in which to rest. Having a fur coat is very useful in the winter but it can be quite a problem in a hot summer.

May 1st

It was raining. It was dark. I was alone. I was frightened. And I was back in the city. I was crouched low behind a collection of dustbins. I could feel my heart beating, and my senses were so heightened that when I heard a slight noise a few yards away to my right I almost jumped out of my skin.

I was back in the city and I was lost and all I wanted was to be back home. I tried to crouch even lower, to melt into the pavement, to become invisible.

I heard the noise again. But now it was getting closer. Slowly, I raised my head a little and peered around one of the dustbins.

Standing no more than six feet away from me was the largest, cruellest looking cat I had ever seen. He had bitter, cruel, wicked eyes and the sort of grin that always means sorrow to someone else. His fur was matted with dirt and oil and as we stared at one another I felt myself shiver involuntarily. I had never before seen any creature who reeked so vividly of evil.

Slowly, I stood up and started to back away. But for every inch I moved back the cat with the wicked eyes moved forwards an inch.

Suddenly, I saw him brace himself ready to pounce. His tail flicked menacingly and the muscles in his hind legs tensed. His eyes were half closed as he concentrated all his evil energies on me.

Terrified, I looked around for an escape route.

My only chance was to slip through a narrow space between the two dustbins on my right and to hope that in the darkness I could put enough distance between the two of us to give myself a chance to find somewhere to hide. I stood up and tensed my muscles ready for my escape.

And then, just as the cat with the cruel eyes started on his leap, I jumped sideways.

At least, I *tried* to jump sideways.

But nothing happened!

My muscles were frozen and I stayed exactly where I was, as solid and as unmoving as if I had been turned into a statue or as if, like Lot's cat, I had been turned into a pillar of salt.

The cat with the cruel eyes pounced and I screamed and woke up.

"Everything is all right!" purred Thomasina for the tenth time. She licked the side of my head reassuringly and nuzzled closer to me so that I was comforted by the warmth of her body. I shivered and then murmured a short prayer of thanks to St Gertrude, the patron saint of cats in distress.

It is the fifth or sixth time that my sleep has been disturbed by the same terrible dream. Each time the dream has ended in the same way: with my muscles frozen stiff with fear. And on each frightening occasion Thomasina has comforted me and helped me overcome the terrors of the night.

I wonder if these nightmares will ever stop. Or if they are a mental scar I will carry for the rest of my life.

May 4th

I caught my very first rabbit this morning.
   It tasted very good.
   I like rabbits.

May 7th

Thomasina and I were feeling rather adventurous today and so instead of staying in the garden to hunt we ventured out into the field.

We don't often do this, partly because there is plenty of wild life waiting to be caught within our own private hunting territory but mainly because we both once had an exceedingly unpleasant experience in a field.

We had been hunting and we were both having a light snooze in a field of corn when suddenly a huge monster of a machine came whirring and beating and snarling through the field. It nearly ate us both up!

Ever since then we have both been very wary of fields.

But today's expedition was well worthwhile and we had an extremely successful time. Thomasina caught two voles and a shrew and I gorged myself on two extremely plump and succulent field mice.

Then, suddenly, before either of us had time to cry out to the other, we both found ourselves rolling over and over in the long grass with a well built cat sprawling on top of us.

Our attacker turned out to be a fourteen year old tom cat called Blackie, who lives on a nearby farm.

"What are you doing in my field?" he demanded, gruffly, as Thomasina and I struggled to regain our feet and our composure a few moments later.

We explained who we were, where we had come from and what we were doing in the field.

"This is *my* field!" said Blackie firmly. "You keep out of my field and I'll keep out of your garden."

Thomasina and I agreed that this sounded an amicable and extremely acceptable arrangement and speedily promised to honour it. Blackie the farm cat was huge but didn't seem to have an ounce of unnecessary fat anywhere on his body. He was, as Thomasina so aptly put it later, a furry feline fighting machine. Neither of us wanted to annoy or upset him.

"I used to catch all the food I needed on the farm," said Blackie, rather ruefully. "But it's months since I've smelt or seen a rat there, and a week since I caught a mouse without coming into the field." He seemed a little guilty about his rather brusque behaviour and clearly wanted to explain.

"Don't your Uprights feed you?" Thomasina asked him.

Blackie looked at her and then at me with a puzzled look on his face. "Feed me? Why would they do that?"

"Do you mean that you only eat what you catch?" I asked him, astonished.

Blackie looked very confused. "Of course!" he said, clearly mystified. "Why should my Uprights feed *me*? I don't feed *them!*"

Thomasina and I were astonished to discover that Blackie has been catching all his own meals since he was weaned. To our surprise he finds our way of life as strange and as unreal as we find his.

May 10th

I almost hate it when the Upright in Trousers cuts the grass.

Long grass is far more comfortable to lie on than the short, spiky stuff, and it's far easier to find a mouse or a shrew or a vole hiding in long grass than it is to catch one unawares on grass that has been cut. When the grass is long, small meals cannot see very far, but when the grass is short they have a clear view for yards and yards and yards!

The noise made by the machine used to cut the grass is another annoyance. I wish I could find someone to explain to me how it is that such a small machine can make so much noise. It makes far more noise than a motor car, which must be at least ten times as big.

Where does all that noise come from?

But I don't *quite* hate it when the Upright in Trousers cuts the grass because when he has finished there is always a huge, soft pile of grass cuttings to sleep on. (There are two mysteries about these piles of grass cuttings. First, why do they disappear? Within a week a huge pile of grass cuttings will have shrunk to half the size. Where do all the missing cuttings go? Does someone eat them? And second, why do the grass cuttings gradually get warmer and warmer? I once went to sleep on a pile of grass cuttings in the autumn and woke up with a very hot bottom).

May 12th

Thomasina and I were both snoozing on the landing early this hot morning (it is one of the coolest places in the house) when the peace and quiet of the early morning was shattered by a scream from the Uprights' bedroom.

We were up in an instant and both raced to see what had happened. My first thought was that the mouse which I had lost behind the wardrobe last week had at last emerged. Knowing what butterfingers the Uprights are I didn't want to leave them to catch it.

But there was no sign of the mouse.

Instead, the Upright in Trousers was standing at the bedroom window and the Upright who wears a Skirt was clambering slowly and sleepily out of bed to join him. Clearly full of excitement the Upright in Trousers was pointing out of the window and shouting incoherently.

Desperate to find out what had happened Thomasina and I scrambled between the two Uprights and jumped up onto the window-sill.

"An energetic family of moles had moved into the garden."

We were not surprised that he was excited.

An energetic family of moles had moved into the garden.

Yesterday the lawn behind the house had been as smooth and as smart and as boring as a neatly laid carpet. This morning it had acquired about a dozen very neat and quite regularly arranged mounds of fresh earth – all of which had quite clearly been made by moles.

Like the Upright in Trousers, Thomasina and I were very excited. We both *love* moles. They taste horrible but they do provide excellent sport. We ran downstairs as fast as we could, amazed as ever at the way the Uprights overreact to these things.

We spent a wonderful couple of hours trying to catch a mole before the sun came out and it got too hot for hunting, and although Thomasina almost caught one we were sadly unsuccessful.

When the heat got too much for us we went back into the house for a little light breakfast and then we went for a snooze on the cool earth underneath the mulberry bush.

A few minutes later Thomasina nudged me. I opened my eyes and watched in amazement as the Upright in Trousers appeared carrying a spade and a bucket.

He spent the next hour and a half trying to catch the moles by scooping up the piles of soft earth and putting them into his bucket.

Thomasina and I both looked at one another and smiled, knowing that the moles would be hidden safely underground.

May 14th

I was sitting on the window-ledge of the coach house early this evening when a mouse flew past me.

I think I must have eaten something funny.

May 15th

At twenty past ten this morning I caught my first lizard. It was not a very large one but it was indisputably a lizard.

I had never caught one before and for a few moments I was very proud of myself. My initial plan had been to eat it but I quickly discovered that the lizard had a very thick, leathery skin which made it about as edible as an Upright's shoe. The smell of it was not very attractive either and I strongly suspected that even if I had been able to eat it, the lizard would have been about as tasty as a shrew (and as every cat knows they are even more disgusting than white fish).

So, I decided to take the lizard into the house for a little sport. I was, I confess, also hoping to show it off to Thomasina.

Once inside the house I dropped the lizard and put a paw on it to stop it scuttling away. Lizards don't look very speedy but I had already discovered that they can move extraordinarily quickly.

"Its tail is coming off" said Thomasina, who had rushed to meet me when she had heard me coming in through the cat flap. She knew from the noise I made pushing the small plastic door aside that I was carrying something in my mouth. It's very easy to drop a catch when struggling through the cat flap, so both Thomasina and I tend to go through as quickly as we can.

I will never forget what happened next.

The tail-less lizard ran off towards the fridge and its abandoned tail tried to wriggle off in the direction of the pantry.

I was so stunned that for a second I didn't move, even though I knew that I would have to act quickly before the two parts of the lizard disappeared completely. (There is more wildlife living underneath that refrigerator than there is in the garden and it must be desperately overcrowded there. I bet it's like a miniature wildlife park).

Just then the Upright who wears a Skirt came in. When she saw Thomasina and the wriggling lizard

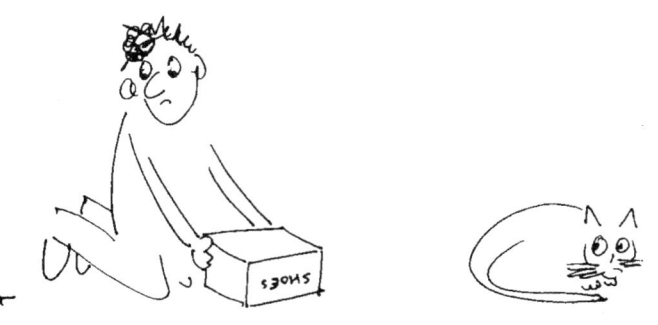

"My heart always sinks when the Upright in Trousers tries his hand at hunting."

and its independently mobile tail she screamed and ran out again. A few moments later she returned accompanied by the Upright in Trousers who was carrying a cardboard shoe box.

My heart always sinks when I see the Upright in Trousers carrying a cardboard shoe box because I know that he is about to try his hand at hunting. I winced inwardly and looked at Thomasina who wearily raised an eyebrow an almost imperceptible amount. We have both learned from experience that there is no point at all in trying to help the Uprights when they are attempting to hunt, so we sat where we were and watched. Nothing is as stubborn as an Upright when he has got a cardboard shoe box in his hands.

First, the Upright in Trousers took a paper handkerchief out of his pocket and picked up the lizard's tail. Then, with quite astonishing speed, the front half of the lizard started to make a run for the door.

Everything happened very quickly. While the Upright who wears a Skirt squealed loudly and pulled her skirt very tightly around her knees, the Upright in Trousers lunged at the lizard with his shoe box and, much to everyone's surprise (including, I think, his own) he caught it.

Finally, while the Upright who wears a Skirt wilfully stopped Thomasina and I from going out through the cat flap, the Upright in Trousers carried the box and the two pieces of lizard outside into the garden.

May 18th

I don't think the Upright in Trousers is feeling very well today.

He went out onto the lawn first thing this morning carrying half a dozen empty milk bottles and a similar number of short canes. He then stuck the canes into the ground and put the upside down milk bottles on top of them.

When he had finished he came back into the house, looking very pleased with himself.

Thomasina and I suspect that this strange behaviour may have something to do with the fact that the moles are still digging up the lawn.

May 20th

Thomasina behaved very strangely all day today. Eventually, I could stand it no longer. I asked her what was worrying her.

"I don't want to tell you," she said. "You'll laugh."

"I won't!" I promised.

She looked straight at me, defying me to laugh, and then told me what was on her mind. "I was sitting outside last night when a mouse flew past me."

I did not laugh. In fact I did not say or do anything. I was remembering the mouse which had flown past me a few nights ago.

"You don't believe me, do you?"

"I do." I said, firmly. And then I told her that I had seen one too.

May 23rd

Although Thomasina and I have been careful not to break our pact with Blackie the farm cat by wandering into the field where he hunts we have both been hoping that we would meet him again. On several occasions we have wandered down to our garden fence in the hope that we might see him.

It was, however, some little time after our first chance encounter before we met him again.

"Hello!" he said, peering through the fence at us. "Don't you two come into the field any more?"

Thomasina and I looked at one another. "You told us not to," replied Thomasina very timidly.

"Don't be silly!" said Blackie. "I don't want you *hunting* in the field but I don't mind you coming in here when you fancy a bit of a wander."

Thomasina and I were delighted and we immediately jumped up onto the top of the fence and down into the field.

"Are there any more cats down at the farm?" I asked, as the three of us strode off across the field. Thomasina and I had to trot to keep up with him.

"Two kittens and an old Queen called Snowy," answered Blackie. "I take them what I can: mice, rabbits in the season, that sort of thing."

"Are there any dogs?" Thomasina wanted to know.

"Of course there are dogs!" snorted Blackie. "How else do you think the Uprights keep the sheep under control? They would be running around all day without a couple of dogs to help them."

"Do you get on with them all right?" asked Thomasina, as we tiptoed through a bunch of swaying poppies.

Blackie looked puzzled. "Of course!" he said, without hesitation. "Whenever there are a cat and a dog living together the cat is always the boss. It's understood."

Blackie told us that he had never met a dog he would not be happy to fight, and because dogs always instinctively knew this he had never met a dog he *needed* to fight. "They're all noise!" he said. "They're good at barking but that's about it. Back a cat into a corner and he'll fight to the death, but back a dog into a corner and he'll usually end up whimpering and running off with his tail between his legs."

We both got the feeling that Blackie did not have a high opinion of dogs.

May 27th

Isn't it strange how most of the barriers to success exist within our own minds?

Up until this month I had never really got down to catching a rabbit. And to be honest I had given up. I didn't think that I would ever be able to catch a rabbit.

But my success a few weeks ago seems to have changed my luck or my confidence or both. During the last four days alone I have caught three more rabbits!

When I told Blackie about this he said that our faith in our ability to succeed is influenced not only by our own successes but also by the achievements of others.

He told me that a few years ago the record for the number of mice caught locally in one year had stayed at 199 for as long as any cat could remember.

"The number 200 had become an invisible barrier," he explained. "No one thought it could ever be bettered."

And then, Blackie explained, a young tom who had come into the area with some new Uprights caught 242 mice in a single year.

"I don't think he knew about the previous record," said Blackie. "He just set about catching as many mice as he could without any limits on his imagination or his expectations."

According to Blackie the only significant thing about this was that it removed the invisible barrier which had been holding back other cats – some of which were much better hunters than the newcomer.

"During the following twelve months," Blackie told us, "four cats caught over 200 mice. And the year after that seven more broke the "impossible" barrier."

Blackie said that the more we think something is impossible the more impossible it becomes.

June 2nd

I was sunning myself on a large, flat, steel grey rock that stands at the back of the garden rockery when I heard a clumsy rustling noise in the primulas on my left.

Without having any idea what was there I pounced blindly and a moment later found myself clutching a small, stumpy little lizard that had no tail.

It was, I realised immediately, the same lizard that I had caught a short while ago. The Upright in Trousers, who had carried it outside in his shoe box, must have lost it again.

"I dropped the lizard into one of the Upright in Trousers' rubber boots."

Most of the time I find it difficult to think of ways to repay the kindness of our Uprights. They are always there when we need them. They open doors and windows when we want them to and never forget to feed us. They are loving and generous friends.

So, I welcomed this opportunity to help repay a little of their kindness by recapturing the lizard and taking it back into the house for them. The Uprights were out, so when I got indoors I jumped up onto the shelf in the lobby and dropped the lizard into one of the Upright in Trousers' rubber boots where I knew it would be safe.

June 7th

Thomasina and I caught a mole each today and I can't remember ever seeing the Upright in Trousers look so pleased.

We left the bodies on the back door step, and when the Upright in Trousers saw them he gave a strange little whoop of joy before coming over and stroking us and tickling us under our chins.

He then went over to the fridge and took out a large piece of chicken which he gave us to eat. We were very grateful because pulling moles out of the ground is hard and tiring work.

But Thomasina, in between mouthfuls of chicken, did admit that she will never, ever understand Uprights.

June 12th

I saw a vole on the other side of the stream this morning and tiptoed through the water to get to it. Unfortunately, the vole got away but I was surprised to find that the water was not anywhere near as unpleasant as I had thought it would be. In fact it was delightfully cool and surprisingly refreshing. I could quite get to like it.

June 14th

I am mortified! I was caught paddling in the stream!

It was boiling hot, and I was beginning to envy the sheep who have all their fur shaved off for the summer months when I remembered how cool and refreshing the stream had been the other day. I wandered over and after a few moments hesitation jumped straight in.

I had intended to stay in the water for no more than a minute or so but I found it so pleasant that I quite forgot myself and splashed about for positively ages.

Suddenly, to my absolute horror, I looked up and saw that both the Upright in Trousers and the Upright who wears a Skirt were standing on the bank staring down at me with incredulous looks on their faces. I hurriedly clambered out onto the bank and concentrated hard on licking my tail in the rather forlorn hope that the two Uprights would be convinced that they had been imagining things.

I'm afraid I don't think my ploy worked.

June 17th

I was lying, half asleep, in the bedroom this morning when Thomasina wandered in looking very sorry for herself.

"I met Blackie," she explained, when I asked her what had upset her.

I was surprised. "I thought you liked Blackie."

"I did," replied Thomasina, rather sulkily, making it perfectly clear that whatever good feelings she had about Blackie were now of purely historical interest.

I moved a few inches to one side so that Thomasina could lie down on the bed beside me. "What happened?"

"I was sitting on the gate when I saw him coming along the lane," explained Thomasina, who was clearly quite upset. "I said "hello" but he just spat at me."

"Why on earth did he do that?" I asked, surprised. It didn't sound like a thing that Blackie would do.

Thomasina just shrugged.

"You must have annoyed him!"

"I haven't done *anything* to annoy him," insisted Thomasina. "In fact yesterday I helped him find his way back down that huge oak tree behind the shippen." She sniffed. "A fine thanks I got for my trouble."

I couldn't help smiling. "Blackie was stuck up an oak tree?"

Thomasina nodded. "You know how tricky that tree is. It's easy to get up into the branches, but getting back down can be very difficult."

"And you had to help him down?"

"I showed him that route we worked out when we got stuck."

"You mean the route *I* worked out when we got stuck?"

Thomasina did have the good grace to look just the slightest bit embarrassed. She nodded.

I couldn't help laughing. Thomasina just doesn't understand tom cats at all. "I'm not surprised that he spat at you!"

Thomasina looked puzzled. "I thought he would have been grateful," she said. "I don't see why anyone should be annoyed at someone who has helped to rescue them."

I reached out a paw and gently touched Thomasina on the back of her neck. I do love her very much but sometimes I marvel at her innocence. Occasionally, I think it is her most endearing quality.

"You must *never* expect male cats to be grateful when you have helped them," I explained to her. "The more you do for them the more resentful they are likely to be – particularly if, like Blackie, they are rather independent and desperately proud of their self sufficiency."

Thomasina frowned. "But that's silly!" she protested. "Why should Blackie be resentful because I helped him?"

"Because the fact that you had to help him showed up a weakness and affected his own self image," I explained patiently. "When Blackie saw you this morning he was reminded not of your kindness in helping him down from the tree, but of his own incompetence and stupidity in getting stuck in the first place."

"Hmmmm!" said Thomasina, thoughtfully. "When you put it like that I suppose I was lucky only to be spat at. The next time I see a tom cat stuck up a tree I'll make sure that I leave him there."

June 19th

The Upright in Trousers cut the grass again today.

I wonder why he does it?

He always moans and gets terribly upset when the noisy machine he uses fails to start (as it invariably does).

And the moment he has finished, the grass starts to grow again! Within a week, or two at the most, it will be the length it was before it was cut.

It isn't as if he does anything useful with the grass he has harvested. He just puts it all in a pile at the bottom of the garden and forgets about it.

Cutting the grass is one of those strange rituals which Uprights seem to take very seriously but for which I can see absolutely no purpose.

June 20th

I caught one of the flying mice this evening.

I was sitting on the coach house window-ledge when it flew past a couple of inches away from the end of my nose. Without even stopping to think about it I leapt off the ledge and caught the mouse in mid flight.

I took it into the house to show Thomasina, but when I put it down for a moment while I called to her the thing flew away!

June 21st

I caught Stumpy the lizard again today, though heaven knows how he escaped from the rubber boot and got back out into the garden. I have a growing respect for him. He seems to be a real survivor.

June 22nd

There was quite a commotion in the house today.

The Uprights saw my flying mouse and were clearly as confused and startled by it as Thomasina and I had been.

I do not think I have ever heard the Upright who wears a Skirt scream quite so loudly. She ran out of the house clutching her hair when she saw the flying mouse.

June 26th

Blackie says that flying mice are quite common around here. He says they are called bats and that no one bothers to catch them because they are quite inedible.

June 27th

I caught a field mouse very early this morning and took it upstairs for a little quiet hunting practice. I'm rather embarrassed to admit this but it has been rather a long time since I caught a mouse and I suspect this is because my hunting skills badly need sharpening.

But, while chasing the mouse around the bathroom, I collided with a small table holding an impressive array of bottles and jars. The table didn't fall over but quite a lot of the bottles fell off and crashed onto the floor.

The noise they made must have woken up the Upright in Trousers because a few moments later he burst into the bathroom looking very dishevelled. His hair was standing on end, he had a dark, stubbly growth on his chin and his pyjamas were badly crumpled. How do Uprights do it? When Thomasina and I wake up in the morning we look just as elegant as when we went to bed. But when the Uprights get up they always look a real mess.

I feel distinctly embarrassed about what happened next.

While I stood still and did nothing the Upright in Trousers emptied out the metal waste-basket which stands in a corner by the sink and trapped the mouse underneath it. My mouse! Without a word of apology or explanation!

I stood around for a while, ready to recapture my prey, but I was wasting my time. The Upright in

"The Upright in Trousers burst into the bathroom looking very dishevelled."

Trousers slid a magazine underneath the waste bin and then took the bin, the magazine and the trapped mouse out of the bathroom and down the stairs. It was the last I saw of it.

June 28th

I was too depressed to eat breakfast this morning.

"What's the matter?" demanded Thomasina, as she licked her whiskers after finishing off all the food that the Uprights had put out for us both. "Are you off your food?"

I explained what had happened. I told her about the mouse the Upright in Trousers had taken from me. And I explained that I really didn't have an ounce of self confidence left.

Sometimes I complain about Thomasina.

I have been known to go on about her faults and, among other things, to accuse her of being greedy.

"Thomasina is a real friend."

But no one could ask for a better friend. When things are difficult Thomasina is a real pal.

She told me about some of her own most embarrassing experiences and she cheered me up no end by making me laugh. By the time she had finished I felt a good deal better.

"There's no point in crying over a lost mouse," she insisted. "There are plenty more mice in the skirting boards!"

And she was right, of course.

On occasions like this I always realise just how important friendships are. As the years go by we all meet many, many cats. Some are no more than vague acquaintances. A few we will think of as friends.

But none of us make more than a few *real* friends. And none of us make *real* friends quickly or easily. Such relationships take many months, even years, to develop fully. But, once developed, real friendships last a lifetime and provide us with support, succour and encouragement at the times when we are most lonely and vulnerable, and at the times when we most need support, succour and encouragement.

In my view real wealth is measured not in expensive collars or beautifully made wicker baskets, nor in plaid rugs or expensive toys, but in friendships.

Thomasina is my very best, very dearest, very closest friend.

June 30th

Today I spent an hour watching a thrush trying to break open a snail's shell in order to get at the meat hidden inside it.

Time and time again the thrush picked up the snail and dropped it onto a stone. And each time the snail's shell remained unbroken.

But the thrush did not give up. It must have repeated the procedure forty nine times.

On the fiftieth attempt the snail's shell broke and the thrush was able to get at its lunch.

The fiftieth drop was no different to the forty nine drops that preceded it. The snail dropped no further. And yet the shell broke.

Life is sometimes very curious.

July 2nd

Thomasina and I were out in the garden when we both had the fright of our lives. A huge noisy bird as big as a house and noisier even than the machine the Upright in Trousers uses to cut the grass flew over and only just missed the chimney pots.

Thomasina was so alarmed that she squeezed right underneath the oil tank. I ran indoors intending to hide in the cellar but collided with the Upright who wears a Skirt who was hurrying out of doors to see what had made the noise. She tripped and fell over dropping the bundle of clean washing that she was carrying. It all landed right on top of me.

"It took the two of us nearly an hour to entice Thomasina out from underneath the oil tank."

It took me an age to disentangle myself from a confusion of bewilderingly complicated clothes, and it then took the two of us nearly an hour to entice Thomasina out from underneath the oil tank. When she did finally emerge she was covered in dust and cobwebs and she reeked of oil. It took her most of the rest of the day to lick herself clean.

I feel sure that if these big birds knew just how much chaos they cause they would fly a little higher or, at the very least, make an effort to avoid flying directly over houses.

July 6th

The two Uprights, Thomasina and I, went for a walk today.

We went diagonally across the field that lies at the bottom of the garden and all the way down to the stream. The grass in the field is now very high and the scent of wild flowers was so strong that poor Thomasina started sneezing and had to be carried. That was a pity because it meant that she missed the wonderful smell of mice, shrews, voles and other food with which the field was liberally laced.

When we got to the stream the Upright in Trousers took off his shoes and socks, rolled up his trouser legs and went paddling in the clear water in his bare feet. The Upright who wears a Skirt laughed a lot but after a while she slipped off her sandals and sat on the grassy bank dangling her feet in the clear, sparkling water.

To begin with, Thomasina and I sat on the bank with her and just watched the Upright in Trousers but after a few minutes my attention was caught by a rustling in the grass on the other side of the stream. (Why, I wonder, do all the most exciting rustlings take

"The Upright in Trousers took off his shoes and socks, rolled up his trouser legs and went paddling."

place on the *other* side of the stream?) Desperate to see what it was I jumped down into the stream without really thinking about what I was doing.

It was not, of course, the first time I have been "paddling", but the Uprights seemed very surprised and both clapped their hands in delight.

Sadly, when I got to the other side of the stream I discovered that the rustling I had heard had been caused by a grasshopper. I have eaten them before and they have always made me sick so I left it alone. I sat in the sun on the other bank for a few minutes to let my fur dry and then, when I was ready, got the Upright in Rolled-Up-Trousers to carry me back across to where Thomasina and the Upright who wears a Skirt were sitting.

Thomasina said that she had wanted to cross the stream with me but that she had got cold feet. I told her that if she had crossed the stream then she really would have had cold feet.

July 9th

Another beautiful, sunny day.

Thomasina and I had planned to go into the wood to look for voles. But it was too hot to do any hunting so we stayed in the garden and slept.

July 12th

When I woke up this morning it was so hot that I could hardly breathe. Having a fur coat is all very well in the winter but it can be something of a disadvantage in the summer. I like the sunshine but the heat is beginning to get me down and I would give a bowlful of custard for a fresh, cool autumn morning.

July 15th

It rained all day.
   What a pity.
   I hate it when it rains.

July 20th

Last night I think I exorcised the evil spirit of the Cat with the Cruel Eyes.

I had my horrible nightmare again.

But this time I didn't freeze.

When the time came for me to escape I ran like the wind and when I looked behind me the Cat with the Cruel Eyes was nowhere to be seen.

I really do think that I have put this nightmare behind me now.

July 27th

Our Uprights had visitors today.

Unfortunately the visitors brought with them two Little Uprights who seemed determined to derive pleasure out of chasing Thomasina and I around the house and garden.

When, after about an hour or so, I thought I had managed to find a quiet spot behind the potting shed I was rudely awakened by a noise behind me. I turned and found that one of the Little Uprights was trying to tie a tin can to my tail. I got away just before he finished the knot.

I escaped by climbing up to the top of a gnarled and rather elderly ash tree which stands on the edge of the vegetable garden. The ash tree looks easy to climb, but the lower branches are very brittle and I felt secure in the knowledge that if the Little Uprights tried to follow me their weight would prove too much.

I was right.

The first Little Upright to try to climb the tree soon ended up flat on his back, clutching a piece of broken branch and bawling pitifully. I stayed up in the tree and was, I confess, slightly disappointed to see him get up and limp away towards the house. I couldn't help noticing that when he got near to the house his limp became far more noticeable.

Moments later I looked down from my vantage point and saw the second Little Upright creeping up on Thomasina who was lying asleep in a sunny spot on the lawn. The Little Upright was carrying a pair of scissors.

"I turned and found that on of the Little Uprights was trying to tie a tin can to my tail."

I miaowed a loud warning and Thomasina turned just in time.

I have an awful feeling that the Little Upright had intended to cut off the tip of Thomasina's tail!

Thomasina was so angry that she lashed out with her claws open and managed to scratch the Little Upright on the hand.

Predictably, the Little Upright ran off into the house screaming.

A couple of minutes later the Upright in Trousers came out. Although he started to tell Thomasina off very sternly I noticed that when he saw the scissors lying on the grass where the Little Upright had dropped them most of his anger seemed to evaporate.

The Little Uprights didn't come out of the house after that, and at tea-time the Upright who wears a Skirt brought our meal out to us so that we could eat in the garden.

After I had eaten I peered in through the living room window and saw that both Little Uprights were sitting, quiet and apparently transfixed, in front of the television set. The television is still something of a mystery to me but its ability to silence Little Uprights means that I have great affection and respect for it. Nevertheless, Thomasina and I decided to take no chances. We stayed outside in the garden.

Later, when the visitors had gone, both our Uprights came and found us and brought with them a plateful of meat. I may be wrong but I got the feeling that they were rather ashamed of the way the Little Uprights had behaved and were, in their own way, trying to make up for it.

July 29th

Looking back in my diary I am embarrassed to see that I moaned about the sunshine and that I said I would like some cool, autumnal weather.

It serves me right, I suppose, but when I woke up this morning I was rather depressed to find that the sky was uniformly grey and that there was absolutely no sign of the sun.

Thomasina said that we should enjoy grey days. She said that without grey days we would not appreciate the sunshine and we would not realise just how special and delightful sunny days can be.

She is probably right, but it does not alter the fact that I prefer sunny days.

August 1st

Every evening the Uprights give us little round crunchy things for our supper.

I like the taste of them but am quite fed up of the shape.

I do sometimes wish that the Uprights would show a little more imagination when buying food for us.

August 4th

I was lying in the garden, basking in the sunshine, when I suddenly and inexplicably found myself thinking about Ginger.

It seems strange and sad to realise that I will almost certainly never see him again. I wish that I could show him round my house and garden. I am very proud of my home, and few things would give me greater pleasure than to try to repay some of his kindness and hospitality.

As I lay there daydreaming Thomasina came up to me and wanted to know what I was thinking.

I don't know why I did it but I told her that I was not thinking about anything in particular.

August 6th

The Uprights gave us little diamond shaped crunchy things for supper tonight. I wonder why?

We usually have round ones which I like very much.

I am not at all sure about the diamond shaped ones.

I do wish the Uprights would stop experimenting with our food.

What do they think we are? Guinea pigs?

August 7th

I caught Stumpy the lizard again today. He seemed very well.

August 14th

At last!

The Uprights have bought Thomasina and I two dishes so that we no longer have to choose between cramming our heads into the same bowl or taking it in turns to eat.

When the Upright who wears a Skirt put down the two new dishes she seemed to have already made up her mind which dish she wanted Thomasina to use and which one she wanted me to use.

"*The Uprights have bought Thomasina and I two dishes so that we no longer have to take it in turns to eat.*"

"The red one is for you, Thomasina," she announced, gently nudging Thomasina towards one of the dishes. "And the blue one is for Alice."

I can see that in future this is going to lead to great confusion, because although the Upright who wears a Skirt can apparently differentiate between the two dishes they seem identical to me. She can see colours but I can't.

The two dishes both smell the same. They are both the same size. They are both the same shape. And they both look exactly the same.

Thomasina was clearly very puzzled. "Can you see any difference?" she asked me.

I shook my head.

"Neither can I," replied Thomasina.

Thomasina said she doesn't care what dish she eats from as long as it is filled regularly with fresh food (and preferably none of that nasty cheap stuff that the Uprights sometimes try to get us to eat).

August 19th

I caught two mice and a vole. The smallest mouse was sweet and tender. The largest mouse was tough and chewy. The vole was, of course, inedible.

August 24th

The four of us (the Upright in Trousers, the Upright who wears a Skirt, Thomasina and myself) had all settled down for a quiet evening in front of the fire (it had been another cold, grey, unsummery summer's day) when the doorbell rang.

For a few moments I thought that the two Uprights were going to have the courage to ignore it. But they didn't. Uprights seem to have difficulty in ignoring bells. They must be programmed to respond to them at some very early age. Whenever they hear a bell they always respond. It does not matter what they are doing or how inconvenient the interruption may be.

It is not unknown for the Upright who wears a Skirt to get out of the bath to answer the telephone and I have lost count of the number of times I have seen the Upright in Trousers drag himself away from the dinner table simply in order to speak to someone at the other end of the telephone.

The visitor was a stranger and he carried a cheap, black plastic briefcase.

"... *both the Upright in Trousers and the Upright who wears a Skirt were bored stiff.*"

At least, he was a stranger to Thomasina and I, and I am sure that he was a stranger to the Uprights too.

They pretended to be pleased to see him. But I could tell that they weren't.

The Strange Upright with a Cheap Briefcase looked very smart in his grey suit, red tie and white shirt. He had two pens clipped to his breast pocket.

The Upright in Trousers brought him into the living room with a marked lack of enthusiasm and the Upright who wears a Skirt welcomed him with a very thin smile. She did, however, offer him a cup of coffee.

That's another funny thing I have noticed about Uprights. Whatever the circumstances, and however unpopular the visitor, the first thing they do is put on the kettle. It is something of a ritual with them.

They are servants of the bell and slaves to the kettle!

I don't know why the Strange Upright with a Cheap Briefcase had called but within minutes he had spread a variety of brochures and leaflets all around the living room and both the Upright in Trousers and the Upright who wears a Skirt were concentrating hard studying them. I am sure I must be wrong, but from where I was sitting most of the brochures seemed to contain nothing but photographs of window frames! The brief snatches of conversation which I bothered to listen to seemed to be about something dull called "double glazing".

The Strange Upright with a Cheap Briefcase stayed for hours and hours and hours, and long before he had gone I could tell that both the Upright in Trousers and the Upright who wears a Skirt were bored stiff. They were struggling hard to suppress yawns and they both looked very miserable.

The unwanted visitor went in the end, of course.

But by then the fire was nearly out and the mood was ruined. An unexpected and unwanted visitor had spoiled what could have been a perfect evening.

My Uprights are strange. They will hardly ever admit to being bored by other Uprights. They will certainly never tell someone they don't like that they find his company less than enchanting. My Uprights would rather put up with six hours of tedium than have to face thirty seconds of mild embarrassment.

But I love them very much.

August 27th

I very nearly caught the mouse who lives behind the greenhouse this afternoon. He is a plump, cheeky little fellow who has the luck of the devil. I had been crouched behind a towering pile of earthenware flower pots for so long that I had cramp in my right hind leg, when I suddenly saw him slip out from a small hole in the brickwork and start to nibble at a packet of seeds that had been dropped on the floor. He picked up the packet, bit off the end and then tipped out the seeds.

"The peace and quiet of the greenhouse was shattered. The towering pile of flower pots had fallen over."

Carefully and slowly I crept forwards until he was within leaping distance. He was so engrossed in what he was doing that he had no idea I was there.

Suddenly, the peace and quiet of the greenhouse was shattered by a loud crash. The towering pile of flower pots had fallen over.

I turned for a moment to see what had caused the crash and when I turned back the mouse had gone! Only a few scattered seeds showed where he had been.

Life is full of disappointments.

September 3rd

I was dreaming about the plump mouse who lives behind the greenhouse when I suddenly woke with a start.

Thomasina was in trouble.

Like all cats, both Thomasina and I have a well developed sense of telepathy, though we only ever use it when we really need to. Every cat in the world can use the telepathy wavelength in an emergency, but we all know that if we use it for trivial messages we will not be able to get through when we really need to.

The system would quickly get blocked if thousands of cats were sending out messages like "I've found a nice plump mouse behind the garden shed – hurry over and help me and I'll share it with you".

So we don't use it unless we really have to.

I didn't use telepathy when I was lost in the city partly because I knew that Thomasina couldn't possibly help me and partly because I knew that nothing I could tell her could possibly stop her worrying. Moreover, I was also conscious of the fact that sending out random "help" messages on the telepathy wavelength can be dangerous. I have heard that there are some unscrupulous cats who will take advantage of a cat in trouble.

But there was no mistake about this: Thomasina was in deep trouble and she was not very far away.

I miaowed loudly enough to wake the Upright in Trousers (it's almost impossible to wake the Upright who wears a Skirt), and without waiting for him to respond I leapt off the bed, ran down the stairs at full speed and shot outside as though my life depended upon it. I knew instinctively that Thomasina was in the nearby woodland and I knew that she was in terrible distress.

I found her lying stretched out in a dark, moss covered hollow. Her right hind leg was caught in a metal trap. It was a terrible, terrible sight. When she saw me she raised her head and cried out so pitifully that my heart almost broke in two with the pain. I wished it had been me who had been caught in the trap. I would, I think, have found it easier to cope with the physical pain than I found it to cope with the sight of my dearest friend in such distress.

I moved forwards and kissed her lightly on the forehead, then I edged round to examine her leg. The trap, a rusty old metal thing, had bitten through the fur and flesh of her leg and I could see the white of her bone through the wound. I wanted to look away and had to steel myself to examine the wound to see how bad it was.

It was bad enough, but things could have been worse.

When the trap had been sprung it had, in addition to Thomasina's leg, caught a piece of broken branch in its jaws. The branch had stopped the trap from shutting as tightly as it might otherwise have done. Thomasina's leg was badly cut but it didn't look to me as though it had been broken.

As I gently licked the fur around Thomasina's injury, to clear away some of the dirt and to allow a little fresh blood to wash the wound clean, I heard the Upright in Trousers calling to me. I stopped what I was doing, told Thomasina that I would be gone only for a few moments, and raced back towards the house.

The Upright in Trousers was standing on the small slabbed area outside the back door. He was wearing an oiled jacket and a pair of mud splattered green wellington boots and he held a large rubber cased torch in his right hand. He was waving the torch about as though searching for something. He had not stopped to change out of his nightwear and in the gap between the bottom of his coat and the top of his boots I could see the blue and white stripes of his pyjama trousers. He looked puzzled and slightly alarmed, and was peering anxiously out into the darkness.

I stood on the edge of the lawn a dozen yards away and miaowed loudly to attract his attention. When I was sure that he was looking in my direction I turned and started back towards Thomasina. Every few steps I turned to make sure that the Upright in Trousers was still following me.

When we reached Thomasina the Upright in Trousers gave out a yell of anguish and leapt forwards in horror. Pausing only to jam his torch in between two branches in a nearby tree, so that the beam shone directly onto Thomasina, he knelt down beside her. He touched her face very gently and stroked her head for a moment. I could see that there were tears in his eyes. When he saw exactly what had happened he tried to prise open the jaws of the trap with his fingers but he clearly did not know how to release the trap and the springs were too strong for him to open it by brute force. After struggling for a few moments he suddenly stood up.

He had blood on his fingers and I don't think all of it was Thomasina's.

He told me to stay where I was and to look after Thomasina and then he ran off back towards the house. He left the torch in the tree and long after I had lost sight of him I could hear him crashing blindly through the trees and bushes and occasionally shouting out in anger as a branch caught him on the face or as he half tripped over a superficial root.

He came back just a few minutes later carrying an armful of metal tools and another huge torch. This time he put the torch down on the ground beside Thomasina so that the beam shone directly onto her trapped leg. Then he used a thick metal bar to force open the trap.

Once he had freed Thomasina he allowed the trap to slam shut again on the metal bar. He was about to hurl the whole thing far off into the woodland when he suddenly stopped and put the bar and trap down next to his other tools. Then he very carefully picked Thomasina up and cradled her in his arms. Using the torch to light his way he walked back to the house as quickly as he could. I hurried back alongside him.

When we got there lights were blazing everywhere and the Upright who wears a Skirt was waiting for us with a bowl full of hot water that smelt of antiseptic. Carefully and tenderly she bathed Thomasina's leg, stroking her and talking to her while she worked. I sat nearby and watched. The Upright who wears a Skirt had hardly finished what she was doing when the doorbell rang. Before anyone could go and answer it the Upright who smells of Antiseptic came striding into the kitchen carrying his huge black bag. He looked very purposeful and businesslike, and I am slightly startled to have to admit that I was very pleased to see him. He stitched and sprayed Thomasina's wound, gave her an injection and told her how lucky she was that nothing was broken. He said that she didn't have to go into hospital but that she had to take things easy for a few days. Then he wrapped a bandage around her leg and told the Upright who wears a Skirt and the Upright in Trousers that he would be back the next day to give Thomasina another injection and to change her bandage.

The Upright in Trousers gave the trap, with the metal bar still in it, to the Upright who smells of Antiseptic who tutted and shook his head. He pressed something and released the spring, took out the bar and promised to get rid of the trap. And then he left, and our two Uprights gave us both a bowlful of cream and Thomasina and I curled up together on the kitchen rug. We were too tired to talk but we both felt very grateful that Thomasina's injury was not worse, and we felt full of love for our Uprights.

September 4th

Thomasina spent the day resting. I stayed with her, partly to keep her company, and partly because I didn't much feel like going anywhere or doing anything.

The Upright in Trousers spent most of the day searching through the undergrowth in the wood. He came back to the house with an armful of dangerous looking rubbish, though I don't think he found any more traps.

September 6th

Thomasina is making a splendid recovery. Today she and I went for a short walk around the garden and then slept for several hours on a patch of soft, cool earth underneath the garden bench.

September 9th

Thomasina's bandage has been removed. She spent the day licking her wound. By evening time her tongue was so sore that she could hardly eat.

September 12th

Thomasina and I went hunting in the wood today. It was Thomasina's idea. She said that if she didn't go there soon she would never go back. When I showed some reluctance she reminded me that the Upright in Trousers had been in there picking up everything that could be dangerous.

"Thomasina and I went hunting in the woods today."

I'm glad we went back. I do like the woodland. It is full of meals on legs.

Thomasina caught a shrew and I caught two field mice.

September 17th

The strangest thing has happened!

A large glass bowl full of water has appeared on the dining room table. And swimming around in the water there is a gold coloured fish!

Thomasina and I have decided that the Uprights have bought the fish as a present for us, and that they are keeping it in the bowl so that it remains fresh.

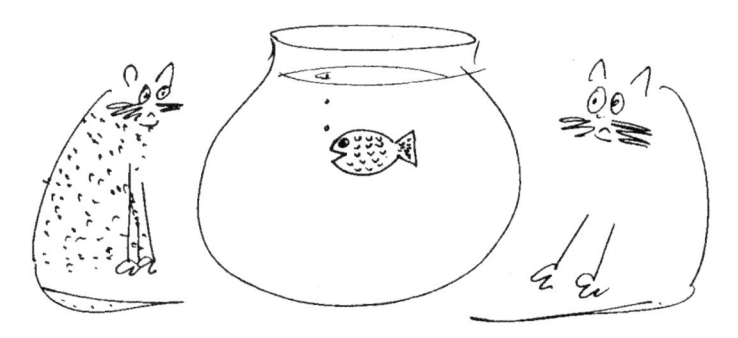

"A large glass bowl of water has appeared on the dining room table. And swimming around in the water there is a gold coloured fish."

September 18th

The Uprights are feeding the fish tiny crumbs which they pour out of a little cardboard container. They are presumably trying to fatten it up but it already looks quite plump. Although I'm not usually keen on fish this one looks exceptionally tasty.

September 19th

The fish is still being allowed to swim around its bowl and the Uprights are still feeding it crumbs. Thomasina and I have decided that the Uprights just want us to help ourselves whenever we feel like it.

We have decided to have the gold fish for lunch tomorrow.

September 20th

Catching the gold fish is not going to be as easy as either of us thought. The glass bowl in which it swims is quite deep and whenever it sees us coming the fish dives to the bottom and stays there.

Thomasina and I spent much of this morning trying to catch the fish but neither of us could reach it.

We are going to have to think of something else.

September 21st

Thomasina has come up with a splendid idea for catching the fish.

She says that if we push the bowl to the edge of the table and then nudge it over onto the floor the chances are that the water – and the fish – will spill out onto the carpet.

Once the fish is out of water it will be as easy to catch as a mouse in a coal scuttle.

September 22nd

We decided to put Thomasina's plan into operation today.

We both climbed up onto the dining table and leant against the glass bowl to push it towards the edge of the table. Although we discovered that the bowl was much heavier and harder to move than either of us had imagined, we eventually managed to start it moving in the right direction.

However, with the bowl no more than three or four inches away from the table edge, the door opened and the Upright who wears a Skirt came into the room.

I have never seen her so angry!

She rushed across the room, swept both Thomasina and I off onto the floor and pulled the bowl back into the middle of the table. Then she proceeded to shout at us so much that we both ran out into the garden and hid. She seemed almost hysterical.

Sometimes Uprights puzzle me.

Why did she get so upset? Why did she care about a fish – and a small one at that?

And why on earth did they put a plump looking fish in a glass bowl on the dining room table if they didn't want us to eat it?

September 23rd

The Upright who wears a Skirt obviously feels guilty about her behaviour yesterday because today she has been quite attentive. But Thomasina and I are still hurt and puzzled.

The dining room door has been shut all day. I wonder if the Upright who wears a Skirt is keeping the fish as some sort of surprise.

September 24th

The gold fish and its bowl have gone!

Shortly after mid-day today the Upright who smells of Jasmine arrived. She brought straw hats, sticks of rock and lots of photographs with her. And when she left, half an hour or so later, she was carrying the glass bowl and the gold fish with her.

When she had gone Thomasina said that she thought that our Uprights might have been looking after the glass bowl and the gold fish while the Upright who smells of Jasmine was on holiday!

What a silly idea!

Why would anyone go to so much trouble for one small fish?

September 29th

Thomasina ate a mole. I told her she would be sick tomorrow.

September 30th

Thomasina was sick.

October 3rd

As winter approaches and the trees start to lose their leaves every warm day is a bonus.

Today the weather was beautiful.

Thomasina and I spent most of the day dozing underneath one of the apple trees in the orchard. The warmth of the sun really does give me enormous pleasure.

I wonder where the sun goes to in the winter?

October 4th

And how does the sun know that it is time to come back again for next year's summer?

October 7th

I saw Stumpy the lizard today. He said he was getting ready to hibernate for the winter. I asked him what he meant and he said he was going to go to sleep until March. I told him I thought that sounded a very sensible idea and that I might try it too.

October 11th

Thomasina has been having a little trouble with the leg she injured. It aches on cold days and is sometimes so stiff that she limps. After she almost fell over for the fourth time she burst into tears with frustration and said how much she hated the Uprights who had left that trap in the woodland.

I told her not to waste her energy hating them, and she soon said I was right and cheered up when I suggested going for a walk in the field to try and find Blackie.

Hate is a damaging and destructive emotion which always seems to do far more damage to the person doing the hating than to the object of the hatred –

who probably doesn't even know that he is hated anyway!

October 14th

The strangest thing happened today.

I was sitting on the window seat in the bedroom when I saw a huge four legged animal arrive at the back door. The animal had a very large head and a long tail. Sitting on its back there was an elderly Upright with a Big Bottom in Tight Trousers.

As I watched the Upright climbed down off the animal, knocked on the back door and was admitted to the house.

When I went downstairs a few moments later I saw the visitor sitting in front of the fire drinking tea with the Upright who wears a Skirt. They were chatting together very cosily.

An hour later, through a crack in the barn wall across the courtyard, I watched as the Upright with a Big Bottom in Tight Trousers climbed back onto the large beast and trotted away as calmly as if nothing untoward had happened.

I have not told Thomasina any of this.

October 21st

Thomasina and I have started storing dead mice behind the boiler. We got the idea from watching squirrels who store nuts for the winter.

"It will be nice to be able to have a mouse in the winter without having to go out into the cold and catch one," said Thomasina, with her usual seductive logic. "Once they have dried out they will be quite tasty."

"We caught three mice today and stored them in a neat pile."

I told her that I prefer my mice to be fresh, but she said that it is not always possible to have exactly what we want and I had to agree with her. If I had my way I would have less white patches on my fur. The white patches get dirty very easily and take a lot of cleaning. Thomasina, being a mackerel tabby is quite fortunate. She can go for several hours without washing and no one would notice.

We caught three mice today and stored them in a neat pile. Thomasina says she thinks we ought to be able to get a hundred mice behind the boiler if we pack them in neat rows.

October 23rd

We now have eight mice, three shrews and two voles in our winter storage area. Thomasina wanted to put a mole in there too but I put my paw down firmly. Moles always make me feel queasy and they always make Thomasina sick.

I was not keen on the voles or the shrews if the truth be known (they are never edible – even when fresh). When the mouse collection gets a little larger I may persuade Thomasina to throw them out.

October 26th

Our collection of mice is looking very impressive, though to be honest I'm not so sure that they are going to be edible in a few months time. We have nineteen of them lined up in fairly neat rows behind the boiler. It has been quite hard work and I do hope that it is all going to be worthwhile. They smell a little but Thomasina says she has heard that mouse meat gets more tender if it is kept a while before being eaten.

November 1st

Disaster!
When Thomasina and I came downstairs this morning we were hit by the most awful smell imaginable. The nearer we got to the back door the worse the smell got and it soon became clear that it was coming from the boiler room.
When we peered round the door we had a terrible shock!
Sometime during the night the boiler had been switched on and had turned our collection of dead mice into a stinking mess of rotten meat. The Upright in Trousers, who was crouching down beside our hoard with a scarf tied over his mouth and nose, was

"Stealthily, Thomasina and I crept outside."

using a small shovel to scrape our roasted mice out from behind the boiler and to put them into a bucket.

Stealthily Thomasina and I crept outside. We stayed outside until darkness fell.

November 5th

When I tried to go out this evening I found that the cat flap in the back door had been barricaded with a tea tray, a large cardboard box and a piece of plywood. I spent a very uncomfortable evening lying on the kitchen floor with my legs crossed.

It was very late and pitch black when the Uprights finally removed the obstacles and I was in such a hurry when I finally got outside that I trod on a slug while looking for a nice soft patch of earth.

I hate slugs.

November 8th

Thomasina and I were both tired this evening and so we went upstairs much earlier than the Uprights.

"I hate slugs."

Although they did not make a lot of noise when they came to bed they woke me up. And the moment I awoke knew that there was another cat in the house.

I don't know *how* I knew. But I did.

I lay there for some time trying to decide what to do. Meanwhile, the Upright in Trousers and the Upright who wears a Skirt both fell fast asleep.

Eventually I decided that I was not mistaken and that I would have to do something. Very cautiously, I woke Thomasina.

As soon as she was awake she knew too.

We looked at one another, carefully jumped down off the bed, and made our way out of the bedroom and along the landing.

We had not gone more than half a dozen paces when I heard the intruder purring in the spare bedroom. I could hardly believe my ears – and nor could Thomasina. Gingerly, we both poked our heads round the door and looked in: sure enough, there, lying on top of the bed was a fat, long haired cat wearing a red leather collar and purring loudly. Underneath the bed clothes there were two large Upright shaped mounds.

Strangers!

Thomasina and I looked at one another, looked back at the strange Uprights and the strange cat, and then very quietly tiptoed back to our bedroom to wake up the Upright in Trousers. We felt confident that he would know what to do.

Thomasina sat on his chest and I licked his ear and when he woke up we jumped down off the bed and looked up at him expectantly. The Upright in Trousers is quite bright and he knows what this means. He yawned, rubbed his eyes, threw back the bedclothes and slid out of bed. Then he followed us along the landing until we stopped outside the spare bedroom. The three of us then peered in through the gap left by the not quite closed door.

But, to our astonishment, the Upright in Trousers just smiled at us, stroked both our heads in that awfully patronising way Uprights adopt when they think they know something we don't, and padded back to bed.

Thomasina and I couldn't believe it. And we certainly were not going to go to sleep with a strange cat in the house. We went downstairs together, ate a few left over crunchy things and then went outside and spent the night sleeping on a pile of old sacking in the potting shed.

What a thing! Forced out of our own home by a stranger.

November 9th

Thomasina and I were cold and stiff when we woke up this morning. The sacking had looked comfortable enough but it made a very poor substitute for soft, warm bedclothes. To make things worse, it was covered in all sorts of insects, many of which burrowed into my fur. It will take hours to get them all out.

As we walked back towards the house I was not sure what to expect. Had we dreamt it? Was there really a strange cat – and a couple of strange Uprights – in the spare bedroom?

We had not dreamt it.

"The Fat Cat sat on the mat."

A strange looking little red motor car that I hadn't noticed before was parked outside the back door, and sitting in the kitchen there were FOUR Uprights: the Upright in Trousers, the Upright who wears a Skirt and the two Strange Uprights.

And right in the middle of the kitchen, sitting on the mat in front of the stove, the fat, long haired cat that we had seen the night before was noisily enjoying a plateful of *our* food!

For a moment neither Thomasina nor I knew what to do. We just sat there and stared in amazement.

The four Uprights all stopped eating and looked at us. The Upright in Trousers called to me and the Upright who wears a Skirt held out a small piece of toast. It was covered in that nice thick orange marmalade that I like very much, but I resisted the temptation to be seduced by it.

The Fat Cat on the mat looked across at Thomasina and I, stared at us for a moment as though *we* were the intruders, and then ignored us and carried on eating!

Thomasina and I turned on our heels and marched out of the room with our heads and tails held high.

November 10th

We stayed outside all day yesterday and steadfastly refused to respond when the Upright in Trousers and the Upright who wears a Skirt came out to call us. They shouted and whistled and made all sorts of promises but we were both quite determined that we were not going back into the house while the Fat Cat was there.

I don't know whether it was just rotten luck, or whether we were both so cross that couldn't hunt properly, but all we caught yesterday were two small shrews and an elderly field mouse.

That just must made things worse, of course.

The shrews were so bitter that we couldn't eat them and the mouse had thin stringy muscles and no fat at all on him. He tasted very rubbery, and if the circumstances had been different I would have given him to the Uprights as a present. To make things worse, it rained all night and the roof of the potting shed (where we had chosen to spend the night) leaks like a sieve. Neither Thomasina nor I slept much, and by the time the sun tried to get up this morning we were both damp, cold, aching, hungry and very bad tempered.

We desperately wanted to go indoors to warm up and get some food, but the little red motor car was still parked outside the back door so we knew that the Fat Cat and his Uprights were still in residence. We were determined not to give in so we stayed outside in the cold and felt truly miserable.

Early on in the day the Upright in Trousers came outside looking for us. He was carrying two bowls full of very enticing looking food and we could tell that he was upset and worried. But he had not had to sleep outside in the potting shed, and so we stayed where we were underneath the rhododendron bush. I secretly hoped that he might hear our tummies rumbling and come and find us and make us eat but he didn't.

"We were both damp, cold, hungry and very bad tempered."

We stayed where we were for an hour or two but the rain got heavier and heavier and started to come through the rhododendron bush leaves so we went back to the potting shed. We must have fallen asleep for a few moments while we were under the bush because someone had been into the potting shed and the two bowls of food were in the middle of the floor. Thomasina said we didn't know for certain that the food had been brought by the Upright in Trousers, and that we could safely eat it without feeling that we had given in.

But who else could it possibly have been brought by?

Besides, the Upright in Trousers knows we always go there when we won't go into the house for any reason.

We ate it anyway because we were both starving hungry and Thomasina said that principles are all very well but you have to eat sometime because if you didn't you would not be strong enough to have principles, and I thought that made sound sense.

After we had eaten we both felt better. We felt stronger and warmer and more determined than ever. And so we curled up on some dry blankets that had mysteriously appeared underneath the wooden bench where the Upright who wears a Skirt does her messing about with plants. And we went to sleep.

When we woke up the little red car had gone.

And when we tentatively peered round the kitchen door we saw that there was no sign of the strange Uprights or the Fat Cat. Slowly and with dignity we went indoors. But before we would even let the Uprights touch us we insisted on checking out the whole house, particularly the spare bedroom.

Only when we were sure that there was absolutely no sign of the Fat Cat or the strange Uprights would we stay indoors. It was good to know that our stand had worked.

Sometimes a cat has to put her paw down firmly.

November 12th

We had chicken for tea. I think this was the Uprights' way of saying "sorry" for having the Fat Cat in the house.

November 14th

Thomasina caught a vole. I told her not to try eating it but she took no notice of me and she was sick all over the hall carpet twenty minutes later.

She insisted that the being sick had absolutely nothing to do with the vole.

November 16th

I nearly caught a mouse. It has been several days since I have had any hunting success.

November 17th

The Upright in Trousers spent the whole day cutting bits off the hedge. Thomasina and I sat on the bedroom window seat and watched him, wondering what he was going to do with so many bits of hedge.

When he had finished, the Upright in Trousers carefully collected all the cuttings together and put them into a wheelbarrow.

Then he wheeled the barrow down to the bottom of the garden.

I watched with increasing interest, desperate to see what on earth he was going to do with all the twigs he had collected.

But I could hardly believe my eyes when he tipped up the wheelbarrow and tried to set fire to all the cuttings he had so carefully collected.

Sometimes I think the Upright in Trousers must be a few hairs short of a fur coat.

But I love him dearly nevertheless.

November 21st

There is a mouse living in the garage. I heard it twice this morning and then caught a glimpse of it this afternoon.

November 23rd

The Uprights were both late getting up this morning. Thomasina and I were very hungry and it was raining outside so we jumped up onto their bed and pretended to fight.

The Uprights soon woke up and it didn't take long to persuade them to get us some food.

November 25th

I caught the mouse that has been living in the garage this afternoon.

It was a cunning little creature and it took a lot of ingenuity to trap it, but in the end I cornered it in between an old oil can and a spare tyre. Then I knocked it out with a clean blow to the top of its head.

Once I was certain that it was unconscious I took it into the house.

I prefer hunting in the house for several reasons.

First, it is warmer.

Second, there are far fewer impossible-to-reach corners for a mouse to hide in.(Apart from the kitchen, which I never use if I can help it because the are far too many tricky impossible-to-reach hiding places).

Third, I don't get as dirty indoors as I do scrabbling about on the floor in the garage or the potting shed.

I hate it when I have spent a tiring afternoon hunting and I then have to spend two hours licking myself clean.

I decided to take this mouse into the bathroom because that really is the safest room in the house for hunting. It is a small room and there are very few nooks or crannies into which a cunning mouse can escape.

But when, with the mouse held firmly between my teeth, I pushed open the door and trotted into the bathroom I had the fright of my life.

One moment the room appeared empty and the next the Upright who normally wears a Skirt was standing up in the bath, stark naked and dripping water everywhere. She looked very pink and strangely bald. She was screaming very loudly and desperately reaching for a large white towel that was neatly folded over the nearby wooden towel-rack.

I had not even known that she was there.

I have long been aware of this strange habit the Uprights have of submerging themselves in water and scrubbing themselves with soap and water. I have talked it over with Thomasina and we have decided that they do it because they cannot lick themselves clean. They have very stiff backs and short tongues and could not possibly give themselves a proper wash the decent, hygienic, feline way.

Anyway, the noise she made startled me so much that I opened my mouth and let go of the mouse.

In retrospect I am prepared to admit that this was a mistake.

The mouse was so relieved at being let go that it instantly started to run up and down the bathroom in a desperate search for a non existent hiding place.

And this just made the Upright who normally wears a Skirt scream even more.

I could not stand it. As much as I wanted the mouse I really could not cope with the noise she was making.

"The Upright who normally wears a Skirt was screaming."

    I slipped out through the still open bathroom door, leaving the Upright who normally wears a Skirt screaming, and my mouse running up and down the bathroom in a frenzy of pointless activity.

116

November 30th

I nearly caught another mouse. That makes two (or possibly three) that I have missed in the last two weeks. Despite my success with the mouse in the garage I seem to be losing my touch.

November 31st

It was cold and wet today. Thomasina and I spent the day in front of the stove. I would have slept but the noise of Thomasina purring kept me awake. I wonder why some cats purr so loudly?

I am quite sure that my purring is quiet and does not disturb anyone.

December 1st

I was shocked yesterday when Thomasina complained about my purring.

We were both lying down in front of the fire when she suddenly told me that my purring was keeping her awake!

December 2nd

I very nearly caught a huge mouse today. I cannot possibly have missed it by more than a whisker. What is wrong with me?

"I very nearly caught a huge mouse today."

December 3rd

I have never had a more embarrassing day.

I caught a small shrew in the shrubbery this morning and brought it into the hall for some hunting practice. But I only had the shrew with me for five minutes or so when I lost it.

Keeping low and not moving I looked everywhere. But I just could not see it.

My first thought was that the shrew was just keeping very still. Like most cats I have great difficulty in focusing on stationary objects and can see best when something is moving.

Most small animals seem to know this instinctively and so when they are being hunted they always keep as still as they possibly can. This, I have always suspected, is a consequence of their having a poorly developed sense of fair play.

So, when I saw Thomasina walking towards me, I used a little subtle body language to let her know that I was looking for a prey that I had temporarily lost.

To my astonishment Thomasina paused in mid stride, grinned very broadly and then stopped where she was.

I raised an eyebrow and glared at her. It is normal courtesy for any cat to help a hunter who is having trouble. (The rules of behaviour are actually quite strict. If the hunt is completed successfully the cat who has done the helping will move quietly to one side and wait. The cat who initiated and completed the hunt will then invite the cat who has done the helping to share in the spoils.)

But Thomasina was not helping at all!

I put both my ears back to let her know that I was pretty upset about her behaviour. But not even that seemed to affect her. She just grinned even more broadly.

I was about to tell Thomasina exactly what I thought of her when, out of the corner of my eye, I detected a small movement. I immediately looked down and, just in time, saw the shrew getting ready to make its escape. It had been sheltering underneath my chin!

What humiliation.

I was so horrified that when the shrew did make a run for it I missed it completely. And Thomasina was laughing so much she missed it too.

December 5th

Thomasina keeps telling me not to be upset but how can I possibly not be upset?

I feel totally humiliated. I may never hunt again.

I spent the whole of today sitting underneath the skimmia bush, trying hard to be invisible.

Just to add to the gloom it rained very heavily all day.

December 6th

I saw a plump mouse beneath the oil tank this afternoon. I waited for it to come out, but when it came within catching distance I pounced and missed it.

I am very depressed.

December 7th

Despite the weather I woke in the night feeling hot and clammy.

My sleep was disturbed by a nightmare in which I was surrounded by a crowd of gigantic shrews. There were scores of them, all as big as a rats, and they were gradually creeping closer and closer to me. I wanted to run away but I couldn't move.

Eventually, when the shrews were all close enough for me to be able to smell their breath (it was awful, as anyone who has ever smelt a shrew's breath at close quarters will know) they all burst out laughing.

After I had been awake for a few moments I felt myself going quite cold as another terrible thought hit me.

What if the shrew that had escaped from my clutches chose to boast about its good fortune to other shrews?

This awful thought kept me awake for the rest of the night.

I spent my second day hiding underneath the skimmia bush, hoping that no one would see me.

December 8th

While hiding this morning I felt, rather than saw or heard, something moving behind me. Cautiously, I turned my head and, to my surprise, I saw a shrew wrestling with a berry it had pulled off one of the lower branches of the bush.

It was *the* shrew! The shrew which had hidden underneath my chin. The shrew which had given me nightmares.

For a moment or two I was too frightened of it hearing me to move even my eyes. But slowly it became clear that the wretched little creature was so busy with the berry it had acquired that it had not even seen me.

Moving so slowly that at times even I was not entirely sure that I was moving, I turned first my head and then the rest of my body. Eventually, after what seemed like a long lifetime, I was in a position to pounce. By now the shrew had finished eating its berry and was greedily reaching up to try and pull down a second.

I braced myself. I pushed my paws deep into the soft earth to get the maximum amount of leverage. I crouched as low as I could. I tightened every muscle I could find. And then I pounced. And I completely forgot that I had been crouching underneath the low growing bush.

As my head and back crashed into the lowest branches of the bush everything around me seemed to shake and shudder. Berries rained down upon me and a broken piece of twig scratched the side of my nose.

Not even the greedy shrew could fail to notice all this noise and movement happening above and around him. He looked up, saw me and grinned.

The accursed creature actually had the cheek to *grin* at me!

But I was not finished yet. With pieces of twig and branch still clinging to my fur I pounced again. I put every ounce of energy that I had left into that pounce. I strained every muscle.

And again I missed him.

With what I can only describe as a sneer the shrew picked up another berry between his teeth and started to waddle off towards the lawn. He did not even do me the courtesy of running. Half way across the lawn he stopped, turned and gave me a second chance to see his best sneer.

Stopping in the middle of the lawn was his final mistake.

The buzzard which caught him dropped out of the sky like a stone. The shrew never had a chance. One moment he was sitting on the lawn with a berry in his mouth and a sneer on his face and the next moment he was just another light lunch for a hungry bird.

Under different circumstances I might have been put out at having my prey taken by a bird. But on this occasion I felt nothing but gratitude for the victor, and I was perfectly happy for him to take the spoils.

December 9th

I have spent many hours trying to work out why I failed so miserably in my attempts to catch that shrew.

Am I just getting old? Are my reflexes gone? Are my muscles too weak? Have I become too soft?

Or was it just fate?

Maybe the shrew was predestined to be eaten by a buzzard not a cat.

December 10th

I caught a vole this morning.

Everyone knows that voles are much more difficult to catch than shrews or mice. Indeed, I seem to remember hearing someone say that they are the most difficult of all creatures to catch.

The vole had only got three good legs but it was remarkably mobile.

And I do not think it was quite as old as it looked.

December 11th

When we got up this morning Thomasina and I were both delighted to see that the rain had finally stopped. From inside the house it looked a wonderful day. The air looked especially crisp and wintry.

So, we decided to go for a walk in the field.

We had walked for no more than twenty or thirty minutes when we saw Blackie, the cat from the nearby farm, stalking something that we could not see.

We could see him clearly enough, he looked quite stately and magnificent as he strode delicately and cautiously along in pursuit of some invisible prey. But even though it was winter, the grass was long enough to ensure that we could not see what he was stalking.

We watched in awe as he slowly lowered himself into the crouch position, adjusted his weight distribution, wiggled his bottom from side to side and then leapt forward as though he had been fired from a gun.

At that moment I realised why I had been unable to catch the shrew that had so tormented me. And why those mice had got away.

I had not been wiggling my bottom properly before I leapt!

There has always been much controversy within cat circles about the importance of the wiggle. Some expert hunters claim that it helps ensure a proper distribution of weight, and some say that it gives more accuracy to the pounce. I have even heard some argue that the effect, although measurable, is largely psychological.

Our dear old friend George was very sceptical about the value of the wiggle, but then he was such a good hunter that he could have probably caught his prey if he had leapt backwards. I still miss George and often think of him with great tenderness.

But, whatever the explanation, I felt convinced that this was what I was doing wrong. And I could hardly wait to get back into the garden to try out my theory.

Meanwhile, Blackie had completed his task and we could hear him enjoying his kill. He ate with tremendous gusto and the meal sounded exceptionally juicy.

Thomasina and I kept well out of the way while he ate since we have both always regarded it as bad manners to turn up just after an acquaintance has started eating a kill. We did not want to make Blackie feel under any obligation to offer to share his meal with us.

When the crunching and chewing noises finally stopped Thomasina and I edged forwards tentatively.

And there was Blackie, licking his lips. He raised his head a couple of degrees and smiled at us.

"Why didn't you come and join me?" Blackie asked us. "There was plenty for all of us." He was not in the slightest bit surprised to see us.

"How long have you known that we were there?" asked Thomasina timidly.

"Since just before I caught the rabbit," answered Blackie to our astonishment. He licked his lips and sighed contentedly. "That was very tasty. There's nothing like a nice rabbit!"

He then told us about life on the farm, talked to us about his family and friends and described in close detail several of his recent kills.

I have to confess that both Thomasina and I thought him rather self-centred since at no point did he ask us how we were. In addition, although neither Thomasina nor I said anything at the time, when we got back home we both admitted to one another that we were a little surprised at Blackie's admission that he had known we were nearby when he was eating but had not invited us to join him.

Still, as Thomasina pointed out, not all cats have our breeding and good manners.

December 12th

By the time we got back home yesterday it was raining hard again, and neither Thomasina nor I had found the idea of going hunting ourselves at all attractive. Instead, we spent the rest of the day and the whole of the evening curled up in front of the stove. I wonder why Uprights do not do this more often?

But by this morning I could no longer resist the temptation to try out my theory about the pre-pounce wiggle and so, although it was drizzling, I set off into the orchard where Thomasina said there were plenty of mice.

I am absolutely delighted to be able to report that putting the wiggle back into my pounce has revolutionised my hunting skills.

I caught two mice this afternoon!

I ate one and hid the other in the bedroom as a surprise present for the Upright who wears a Skirt.

December 14th

The Upright in Trousers has a new box shaped machine which he is very proud of. It has a mouth at the front and when he pushes a small plastic gadget into it the air all around the box is suddenly filled with music.

He played with the box continuously all day long and it was so loud that the whole house seemed to vibrate.

The sound and the vibrations were so painful that Thomasina and I had to spend the day outside, even though it was bitterly cold.

I do not think the Upright in Trousers is aware just how sensitive we are to sound. Our hearing is very acute, especially for high pitched sounds. George once told me that we can hear a much wider range of sounds than any other creatures – including dogs. When sounds are very loud, the vibrations they make can make them doubly irritating and twice as painful.

I quite like music as long as it is played quietly.

December 16th

I am convinced that Uprights are much more intelligent than many cats suspect, but their one great weakness is their inability to communicate with one another.

Thomasina and I communicate vocally, of course.(And we have tried to train the Uprights to recognise different vocal patterns when we speak to them, though their hearing is so poor that they are not very good at it. After years of training our Uprights can just about differentiate between a miaow which means "Would you please open the door" and a miaow which means "I would like a little more breakfast, please").

When we are upset or worried we growl, hiss, scream or spit.

"If Thomasina's tail is upright with the tip curled over I know she's pleased about something."

But most of the time Thomasina and I communicate with one another in more subtle, more accurate, more sensitive and speedier ways.

We use body language to speed things up and to enable us to express emotions which are difficult to put into sounds.

If I swish my tail Thomasina knows that I'm cross. If her tail is upright with the tip curled over I know that she's pleased about something. If she arches her back a little I know that she is a quite angry; if she arches her back a lot I know that she is very angry.

We use our ears, eyes, tails, whiskers and fur to express subtle warnings and share our feelings with one another.

Body language is honest and simple and speedy. It is sad that Uprights do not seem able to communicate in this simple but most effective way.

December 17th

An Upright who does not like cats came to visit today.

Thomasina and I always know instinctively when a visitor does not like cats. However much he or she may pretend that they like us they give away their true feelings in a thousand subtle ways.

Thomasina says that Uprights Who Do Not Like Cats find us too independent for comfort. She says that they feel uncomfortable because we cannot be dominated, ordered about and "owned" in the way that many other creatures can be dominated, ordered about and "owned". She says we remind them of their own lack of independence.

I think this may be too subtle. My own suspicion is that those Uprights Who Do Not Like Cats have some simple but indefinable psychological problem.

When we were younger, Thomasina and I were very naughty. We used to tease Uprights Who Do Not Like Cats by leaping up onto their laps, brushing against their legs and generally making a terrible fuss of them. We knew that they would not dare express their discomfort for fear of offending the Upright in Trousers or the Upright who wears a Skirt.

We have grown out of that now.

Most of the time.

December 19th

Thomasina caught two voles today. But I am pleased to say that she did not eat them.

December 22nd

The birds are using the skimmia bush in front of the house as a fast food restaurant. It is most infuriating. When they land on the bush to eat the berries they are often no more than six or seven feet away from us.

Thomasina got very frustrated this morning. And I am afraid that she made a complete and utter fool of herself.

Enticed by a blackbird which kept singing in between courses, Thomasina launched herself up into the air. She managed to get a paw on the blackbird's back, but the bush would not hold her weight and Thomasina fell through the branches onto the ground.

The blackbird, quite unharmed, flew a few feet up into the air, squawked a little to let everyone know how clever he was, and then resumed his meal.

Thomasina and I could stand it no longer. We went back indoors and went to sleep in front of the stove.

There are times in every cat's life when there is no alternative but to accept the inevitable.

December 24th

The Uprights have been very busy all day and seem to be preparing for some sort of feast.

The Upright who wears a Skirt has prepared a large turkey, a chicken, a leg of pork and a piece of ham. She has also prepared enough vegetables to feed a small army and has made two very large puddings.

Thomasina and I are very worried. We suspect that the house will be over-run by strange Uprights tomorrow. We have, therefore, made our own plans.

There are two mice living in the potting shed. We had been keeping them for what I believe the Uprights call a "rainy day".

Whatever the weather is like tomorrow we will be eating mouse for lunch.

December 25th

Thomasina and I awoke early and were surprised to find that the Uprights were already up and had placed small, neatly wrapped packages by our food bowls.

As soon as they saw us the Uprights rushed over and started to unwrap the two packages without even waiting for us to do or say anything. They then opened the two small tins that were in the packages and spooned out a very strange meal which consisted entirely of very small black eggs. The little eggs did not look very appetising but they were, I have to confess, extremely tasty. The only problem was that when we had eaten them both Thomasina and I felt very thirsty.

Once they had watched us clean our plates, the Upright in Trousers and the Upright who wears a Skirt went back to work cooking and preparing food for all their visitors. Neither Thomasina nor I had ever seen so much food. Indeed, we decided that there probably was not going to be enough room in the house for all the Uprights, and we began to get a little bit worried about the sanctity of the potting shed.

Deciding to wait a little while before we set off in pursuit of the potting shed mice, Thomasina and I sat on a shelf in the garage and watched the house to see just how many Uprights did turn up.

Sadly, however, after several hours of waiting only four Uprights had arrived. Thomasina and I felt very sorry for our Uprights. Judging from the amount of food they had prepared they must have been expecting many, many more than four visitors.

We were about to go and hunt down the potting shed mice when the Upright who wears a Skirt came to the back door with a huge plateful of meat. We both ate so much that we did not have the energy to go hunting, and since there were only four strange Uprights – and no Fat Cat – in the house we went indoors and fell asleep in front of the stove.

December 26th

Thomasina and I ate so much today that by tea-time we were almost unable to walk.

But the kitchen table, the larder and the fridge are all still full of left-over food.

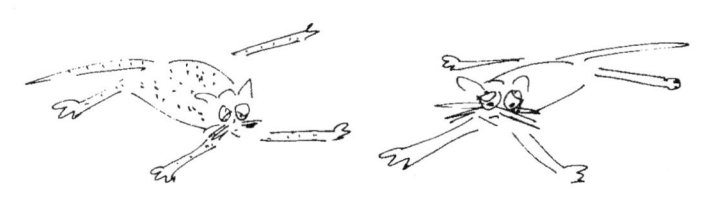

"Thomasina and I ate so much today that by tea-time we were almost unable to walk."

December 28th

Today is the anniversary of George's death.

George was the wisest, kindest, bravest cat who ever lived.

Thomasina and I still miss him. And we will never forget him.

George taught me a great deal.

It was George who taught me that no cat is indispensable.

"Some cats go through life believing that they must always be busy," he said. "They make themselves ill because they are believe that they are quite irreplaceable".

"If you ever feel that," he told me, "leave the room in which you are standing, sitting or lying, go outside and look in through the window. You will see that there is absolutely no sign of you. When you were there you were there. But once you've gone you're gone."

George was, as always, absolutely right.

And his message helps me put things into perspective and remember how unimportant I am.

But some cats are close to irreplaceable. And some cats do leave a void when they leave a room. You may not be able to see where they were, but you can certainly see where they are not.

George was one of those cats.

I would like to think that one day some cats (and, who knows, maybe some Uprights) will think of me that way.

December 30th

Thomasina and I caught the two mice in the potting shed today. They were both disappointingly stringy.

December 31st

Another year is over.
    I do hope that next year is not quite so adventurous.
    Some cats like excitement.

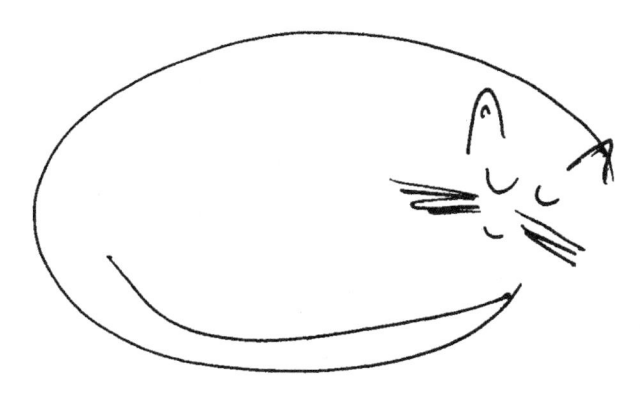

"I prefer a quiet life."

Myself, I prefer a quiet life.

Printed in Great Britain
by Amazon